The Westminster Confession of Faith

John H. Gerstner
Douglas F. Kelly
and
Philip Rollinson

SUMMERTOWN TEXTS
Signal Mountain, Tennessee

First Edition
1992
ISBN: 0-9614303-3-8

Copyright © 1992 The Summertown Company, Incorporated

Library of Congress Cataloging–in–Publication Data

Gerstner, John H.
    A guide to the Westminster confession of faith : commentary / by John H. Gerstner , Douglas F. Kelly, and Philip Rollinson, -- 1st ed.
        p.   cm.
    Includes indexes.
    ISBN 0-9614303-7-0 : $21.95. -- ISBN 0-9614303-3-8 (pbk) : $15.95
    1. Westminster Assembly (1643-1652). Westminster confession.
2. Presbyterian Church--Creeds. 3. Reformed Church--Creeds.
I. Kelly, Douglas, 1943-   . II. Rollinson, Philip B. III. Title.
BX9183.G47 1992
238'.5--dc20   92-8561
                                                            CIP

Printed in the United States of America by Faith Printing Company.

Table of Contents

PREFACE

This work is designed for anyone interested in *The Westminster Confession of Faith*—layman, clergyman, student, professor, generalist, specialist, amateur or professional theologian. It primarily focuses on interpretation and the relationship of the *Confession* to its historical contexts and to our own day. Two of the authors are systematic theologians and the other is an expert in seventeenth-century literature and interpretation. The commentary is based on the Summertown rendering of the *Westminster Confession*, while giving careful attention to the exact wording of the original 1647 text. The commentary follows the organization and format of the *Confession* by numbered chapters and paragraphs, so that one may readily locate the comments on any particular section desired. Quotations from the Summertown version are indicated by upper case.

We would like to express our gratitude to Russ Ragon for his work in preparing the indices.

INTRODUCTION

In order to bring the Church of England into a nearer conformity with the Church of Scotland and other Reformed churches abroad, the Westminster Assembly met at Westminster Abbey from 1643-1646, while the English Civil War was being waged. A distinguished body of Calvinistic scholars, churchmen, and theologians, representing the various religious constituencies from England and Scotland, met with representatives of Parliament, to forge the so-called Westminster Standards: *The Westminster Confession of Faith,* the *Larger* and *Shorter Catechisms*, and a *Directory of Worship*. The goal of a greater Reformed unity throughout the British Empire was realized to some degree during the Cromwellian Interregnum, but it completely collapsed in England with a return to Anglicanism, first with the Restoration of Charles II in 1660 and finally with the establishment of William and Mary on the thrones of England and Scotland in 1689. Nevertheless, the Westminster Standards have endured, especially in Scottish-American Presbyterianism to this day, and are recognized worldwide as a classic statement of Calvinistic theology and Presbyterian church government.

The question now is whether these standards of the seventeenth century still apply or have validity today—a question also asked by many about the Bible itself. This question has many forms. A basic one is historical. It is frequently maintained that cultural values of the past no longer apply to our day. This chronological point is usually joined to an ethnic distinction. Thus, first-century (A. D.) values, it is said, do not apply to the twentieth century, nor do Christian values of the Roman Empire reflected in New Testament writings. They are out-of-date historically and culturally. The Bible's opposition then to homosexuality, for example, is seen by some as culturally-limited and having no relevance to our own more enlightened times.

These two forms of cultural relativism, chronological and ethnic, are widely accepted in our day, particularly among intellectuals, academics, and, alas, yes, clergymen. The belief that human knowledge and understanding are progressive is part of the now thoroughly entrenched concept of evolution. Yesterday's truth must be forgotten in light of today's newer, contemporary truth. The present is assumed always to know better than the past. This view has been powerfully reinforced by the achievements of the ongoing industrial-technological revolution of the last two-hundred years and indeed could legitimately be said to characterize the attitude of Western, modern man. It is this view which has prompted a prominent Baptist theologian, Bernard Ramm, to assert that the old orthodox theology of Christianity can never be adequate in our new age, and so he argues that the so-called new orthodoxy of Karl Barth provides the only way modern Christians can retain their orthodox faith (*After Fundamentalism*, 1983).

A major part of Ramm's relativism is philosophical. About the same time that the Westminster Standards were being formulated, René Descartes was reworking philosophy, detaching it not only from classical foundations but also from medieval, Christian (Scholastic) theology. Modern philosophy, essentially freed from Christianity and practiced almost exclusively by non-Christians, has been pursuing its own ends ever since. Ramm assumes that Christian doctrine must conform to the conclusions of modern, secular philosophy in order to have any contemporary validity [contrary, of course, to Colossians 2.8].

All these forms of skeptical relativism undermine any real belief in the Bible itself and in the contemporary usefulness of a document like the *Westminster Confession*. What they do, of course, is to subordinate the Bible and indeed God, since the Bible claims to be a revelation of Him, to the human intellect. And with that view, the *Westminster Confession* is only useful in the historical, antiquarian sense of showing us what the poor, unenlightened folks back in the seventeenth century thought about God and the Bible. Today, the Bible must be reinterpreted in terms of our intellectual, scientific, and technological advances, and so we are said to need a new formulation of Christianity, like Barth's or someone else's, or lots of new, changing formulations appropriate to the changing times.

But these views, informed by the philosophies of phenomenology are frequently eclipsed by even more radical forms of relativism and skepticism. Existentialism despairs of any meaningful communication or sharing with anyone else even of one's own generation and ethnic group. Thus, as humans, we are cut off from each other and everything else, including God (if there is one), and only have meaningful validation within our own selves and only of ourselves. This secular view has had a tremendous influence on nineteenth and twentieth-century Christianity, reinforcing the pietistic notion that Christianity (or any other religion) is entirely personal and subjective, that it cannot even be discussed meaningfully but only lived out in each individual's consciousness and reflected (dimly) in individual actions.

The Westminster "divines," of course, held no such relativistic opinions. They believed that God is not only the creator of all that exists but is the sustainer of it as well. Consequently He is the ground of all being, who in and of and by Himself establishes both objectivity and subjectivity. They believed that truth is eternal, timeless, and objective, that it is neither culturally, chronologically, nor subjectively distorted, and that it can be objectively apprehended and communicated from one generation to another and from one individual to another. They believed that the Pythagorean theorem could be understood by Frenchmen in 1600 or Julius Caesar in 60 B.C. or anyone of anytime and any culture in precisely the way that Pythagoras understood, conceived, and represented it in the sixth century B.C.

Chapter 1

Concerning Holy Scripture

This chapter is often considered the finest statement on Scripture that the history of the church has produced. It is divided into ten sections, every one of which deserves much fuller treatment than all of them together are going to receive in these brief comments.

1.1 This section defines the essential relation between natural or general revelation and special or Biblical revelation. Theologians often say that God has written two books: the Book of Nature and the Book of Scripture. Both are inerrant as written, but each is capable of being misinterpreted! It is with those two books that this first section deals.

Only the first sentence refers to the Book of Nature and all the rest of the paragraph to the Book of Scripture. In that one sentence, three arguments for general revelation are given: first, OUR NATURAL UNDERSTANDING; second, THE WORKS OF CREATION; and third, PROVIDENCE. Our very understanding itself is an evidence of an understanding source behind us creatures as well as the second, WORKS OF CREATION in general. We ourselves are microcosms in the whole cosmos. Cosmos refers to an ordered universe. It indicates pattern and regularity just as the word "universe" means one world. It, too, points to a single author. When one looks at his own understanding, he sees God reflected there. So much for the static universe, that is to say, our natural understanding and the works of creation in and of themselves alone.

Third there is the story providence tells. We sometimes refer to history as HIStory. A German statement has it that the

Geschichte of the world is the *Gericht* of the world. That means that "the history of the world is the judgment of the world." The Greek word for history, theodicy, also shows God's judgment in the affairs of the universe.

The *Confession* is informing us of these three arguments that everyone can and should recognize. What do they show? They clearly show God's goodness, wisdom, and power. We would be inclined to put these descriptions in the opposite order; power, wisdom, goodness. The first thing that seems to impress a person when he contemplates the cosmos is the fact that only a being existing in and of himself who has the power to bring something out of nothing could possibly be the source of the world. Then when we contemplate that world, we see the wisdom behind its creation and structure. Finally, we notice that this wisdom is bending the universe to our human benefit. It is true, as the poet Reginald Heber says, speaking about nature, that every aspect is pleasing and only man is vile. Even though man is vile, it is at the same time true that this universe is wisely arranged for his benefit. So this goodness of God in a certain sense already appears as a gracious goodness as well.

The one sentence on general revelation comes to this conclusion: THAT HUMAN BEINGS HAVE NO EXCUSE. This statement seems to be true insofar as it refers to men having no excuse for not believing in God, but not quite true enough in that the problem is actually what men do with their belief in God. The *Confession* at this point cites as a supporting Scripture text, Romans 1.20, which not only says, as the *Confession* does, that men are without excuse, but it says that men are not without the knowledge of God. They actually do know God. Their guilt comes in at the point of not worshiping Him as God. So it is not that they do not have an excuse for not believing in Him, but that they do not have an excuse for not worshiping Him in whose existence they do believe (but unsavingly)--"the devils also believe and tremble" (Jas 2.19).

Presumably the reason that the *Confession* puts it this way is that the word belief usually refers to a saving belief. The Westminster divines did not think, any more than the Bible teaches, that men come to a saving belief or faith through general revelation. They suppress that revelation; they hold that truth down; they do not worship the God they know to exist. So they do not savingly believe in Him. At the same time, they do know and in that sense believe in the existence of God – but very reluctantly and with great resistance. They do not actually get Him out of their thinking, although they try continually to do so. If we ask ourselves the question why they do that, we will not get the answer from the *Westminster Confession* until Chapter 6: CONCERNING THE FALL OF MAN, SIN, AND THE PUNISHMENT FOR SIN. In other words, it is because men sin and are fallen in sin that they do not welcome this knowledge they have and are not saved by faith in the God whom they know from general revelation. The Book of Nature, as it were, closes with a guilty mankind left without any excuse for not worshiping God as God. That leads the *Confession* logically to the next statement.

HOWEVER, THESE MEANS ALONE CANNOT PROVIDE THAT KNOWLEDGE OF GOD AND OF HIS WILL WHICH IS NECESSARY FOR SALVATION. Only the revelation of the gospel is the power of God to salvation. In other words, men are damned by the knowledge they have from nature, and only through a knowledge which comes apart from nature will they ever be saved. Something more than natural revelation , as the *Confession* says, is NECESSARY FOR SALVATION.

THEREFORE, IT PLEASED THE LORD AT DIFFERENT TIMES AND IN VARIOUS WAYS TO REVEAL HIMSELF AND TO DECLARE THAT THIS REVELATION CONTAINS HIS WILL FOR HIS CHURCH. So we see that a revelation beyond general revelation is necessary. But the *Confession* says, IT PLEASED THE LORD. That is, it is necessary for us if we are to be saved; it is not necessary for God to save us. If we are to be saved from the damnation of nature, as it were, it is going to be by a revelation of grace. But grace, by definition, is unnecessary. The *Confession* is calling our attention at the outset, to the fact that it is merely the divine good pleasure that accounts for His further and saving revelation of Himself.

The next sentence indicates that this saving revelation was not only supernaturally and specially given to us but that it was supernaturally inspired in writing. Afterwards, IT PLEASED GOD TO PUT THIS ENTIRE REVELATION INTO WRITING SO THAT THE TRUTH MIGHT BE BETTER PRESERVED AND TRANSMITTED AND THAT THE CHURCH, CONFRONTED WITH THE CORRUPTION OF THE FLESH AND THE EVIL PURPOSES OF SATAN AND THE WORLD, MIGHT BE MORE SECURELY ESTABLISHED AND COMFORTED. First, general revelation; second, special revelation; and, third, inspiration. As John Calvin says, when God gave us this special revelation, "He lisped." That is to say, He spoke baby-talk. He condescended to our infantile understanding to make Himself known in His gracious saving role. We may add that He not only did that but He then proceeded to inspire the writing of this baby-talk. That was so that this saving revelation of the truth might be better preserved and transmitted.

We all realize that writing is the only way by which expressions can be preserved for subsequent generations. We know how easy it is to forget and to distort the mere memory of an original statement. So, to preserve and transmit the word of God to the church for all times, this writing was necessary. Notice that the sentence indicates that it PLEASED GOD TO PUT THIS ENTIRE REVELATION INTO WRITING. The *Confession* here does not use the word inspiration, but it uses an equivalent expression. It says plainly that God put this revelation INTO WRITING. We learn before this chapter is over that God used men in the process of putting this revelation into writing. We are informed at the outset that this is God's writing. He put it into writing. It is the same as if He wrote it with His own finger, as Jesus wrote in the dust in the episode concerning the woman taken in adultery, or as God inscribed the Ten Commandments on the tables of stone. These writings are penned by men, but initially they are the writings of God.

One can see how some church fathers have probably injudiciously lapsed into rather extreme language. One pope, Gregory the Great, for example, said that God used these writers as penmen. He did not mean, nor did Jonathan Edwards, who expressed the same opinion, that these men were reduced to inanimate objects or recording machines but that God's use of them, even though they were in full possession of their faculties, was in such a way that they were incapable of error. Otherwise, we could never say that this special revelation is God's writing. If it is God's writing through men, it obviously is communicated without any of man's error being mixed with it. The extreme way of saying that is the way Pope Gregory did actually put it, that God used these men as pens. It is not meant that He did really use them as pens but that what they wrote was as truly God's word as if God had taken up a pen and written it Himself. Nevertheless, the inspired writers wrote as if God had nothing to do with it. That is what Abraham Kuyper meant when he said that a schoolboy could not have written Romans, although Kuyper knew that, were God so minded, He could have made a stone write Romans!

Another reason for this inspired writing is not only to preserve and transmit but that the church should be SECURELY ESTABLISHED AND COMFORTED because of the onslaught of Satan against the church. As our Lord had said to His church, in the world you have tribulation. That tribulation is led by the archenemy of God, Satan. And as Paul teaches in Ephesians, the shield of faith is the word of God. The only adequate protection the church has from the onslaught of the evil one is the secure and certain testimony that the church's life is based on the sure word and testimony of God.

The final sentence not only indicates that the inspired Scripture is necessary for the establishment and comfort of the church but that when God finished lisping the special revelation, He closed His mouth for the rest of earthly history. SINCE GOD NO LONGER REVEALS HIMSELF TO HIS PEOPLE IN THOSE EARLIER WAYS, HOLY SCRIPTURE IS ABSOLUTELY ESSENTIAL. In other words, the Scripture is not only the shield to protect the church from the onslaughts of Satan, but it is the only shield the church is ever going to receive or need. That is what this final sentence adds to this classic opening paragraph. The *Westminster Confession* teaches that we need this shield to protect ourselves from the darts of the evil one and that this is the only shield we will ever have. The canon is closed. God has closed His mouth. He is not going to give us, as long as the world stands, one further word of special revelation. But, as our Lord Himself said, that revelation which He did give us will outlast this world (Is 40.8, Mt 5.18).

So, in summary, we have in Chapter 1, Section 1, a brief but comprehensive statement that God has revealed Himself to all men in the creation and providence of this world and that anyone who does not believe in Him is inexcusable for failing to do so. Because they do fail to do so, however, they need a further revelation of a special kind that God was pleased to give us. Having given it to us, He reduced it to writing, which is our permanent shield against the onslaught of the evil one until Christ Himself comes again.

1.2 The second section can be dealt with very briefly, because it is a mere listing of the canonical Scriptures, the sixty-six books of the Bible. The only reason for the insertion of these by name is to make it crystal clear what this revelation is. This revelation is the totality of special saving revelation and the only protection and comfort of the church while the world stands. It is these books and no other books. After listing them, the Confession simply concludes the section by saying: ALL OF THESE BOOKS ARE INSPIRED BY GOD AND ARE THE RULE OF FAITH AND LIFE.

1.3 Section 3 is equally precise in a negative way. Section 2 tells us what is indeed the one and only special saving revelation of God. Section 3 explicitly rejects another candidate for inclusion in this inspired record of divine revelation, the Apocrypha. The Roman Catholic Church, at the Council of Trent (1546-63) affirmed the Apocrypha as "deutero-cannonical," i.e. that they are a second list of canonical Scripture. So a century later (for the Westminster Assembly finished its work an exact century after the convening of the Roman Catholic Council of Trent) the *Confession* says in Section 3: THE BOOKS USUALLY CALLED THE APOCRYPHA ARE NOT DIVINELY INSPIRED AND ARE NOT PART OF THE CANON

OF SCRIPTURE. THEY THEREFORE HAVE NO AUTHORITY IN THE CHURCH OF GOD AND ARE NOT TO BE VALUED OR USED AS ANYTHING OTHER THAN HUMAN WRITING.

Sometimes, one finds the Apocrypha not only in Roman Catholic translations of the Bible but in some Protestant translations as well. Almost invariably, there will be an indication that these books are meant merely for edification and are in no sense a part of canonical Scripture. Appearing between the closing of the Old Testament canon and the opening of the New Testament canon, they do supply us with valuable information about that intervening period. A great deal of their ethical teaching is highly commendable. Nevertheless, they are not inspired, and they do include many erroneous doctrines as well.

The Apocrypha must be read with critical sharpness if one is to benefit from them, whereas, the writings of God must be read with a determination to let them have "free course" in us. Our Lord used that expression when he rebuked the Pharisees for not letting the word of God have free course in them. He meant that these religious teachers were wresting the Scriptures to their own destruction. The only proper way to read that which God has written is with absolute docility and receptiveness. The Apocrypha or any other non-Scriptural literature, on the other hand, must be read very critically, being evaluated by the normative Holy Scripture. By the same token, the Scripture cannot be read in that fashion if it is once recognized to be nothing less than the word of God. Our one determination should be to let God, Who has been pleased to open His sacred mouth, speak to us by His once-for-all speech in Holy Scripture. This is not only true piety but not to do so is true insanity.

1.4 Now that the *Confession* has taught us that the Bible is God's writing and indicated specifically what are the limits of the canon and what is not included in the canon, it proceeds to make the immediate implication explicit. The reason, it says, that we accept the Bible as authoritative is because of what the Bible is. It is the word of God. Because it is the word of God, it must be recognized immediately as absolutely authoritative. That is the only and the absolutely sufficient reason for bowing before the authority of the Bible–BECAUSE IT IS THE WORD OF GOD, and we recognize it to be so.

This section also indicates why the Bible is *not* to be recognized as authoritative – not because of THE TESTIMONY OF ANY MAN OR CHURCH. In other words, we do not believe the Bible is the word of God because Augustine said so or because Luther said so or because the Protestant Church says it is. This is a flat repudiation of the Roman Catholic viewpoint which insists on quite the opposite. A Roman Catholic is expected to believe that the Bible is the word of God and authoritative because the Roman Catholic Church says it is. One priest has written that if his church said that Aesop's Fables were the word of God and Matthew were not, he would believe that Aesop's Fables are the word of God and Matthew is not. He was stating the orthodox Roman Catholic view.

Benjamin B. Warfield, a great Protestant theologian, has put it this way: the canon is a collection of inspired books; it is not an inspired collection of books ("Introduction" to *Textual Criticism of the New Testament*). That is the way Protestantism speaks. We recognize the Bible for what it shows itself to be, the word of God. Not so, according to Rome. According to Rome, this list of books is recognized as the word of God, because the Roman Catholic church says it is the word of God. In one case you have faith in God and in the other faith in man, specifically the churchmen of the Roman Catholic communion. As you can see, a drastic difference of opinion is involved here, which is clearly expressed by the framers of this article.

1.5 Just as this chapter is the most famous and perhaps the greatest chapter in the *Westminster Confession of Faith*, so Section 5 is probably the most famous and the greatest section in this Chapter. Although it is a fairly lengthy paragraph, it deals with only two subjects. First of all, the *proof* that the Bible is the word of God and, secondly, the *persuasion* that the Bible is the word of God. Not only does it treat these two subjects superbly but its very distinguishing of them is a major contribution to answering the question: how do we know the Bible to be the word of God.

First, we have the proof that the Bible is the word of God. There are no less than ten arguments to prove, show, or evidence its inspiration:

THE TESTIMONY OF THE CHURCH;
THE TESTIMONY OF THE BIBLE TO ITSELF;
THE SPIRITUAL SUBJECT MATTER;
THE EFFECTIVENESS OF ITS TEACHING;
THE MAJESTY OF ITS STYLE;
THE AGREEMENT OF ALL ITS PARTS;
ITS UNIFIED AIM FROM BEGINNING TO END
  (TO GIVE ALL GLORY TO GOD);
THE FULL REVELATION IT MAKES OF THE ONLY
  WAY OF MAN'S SALVATION;
ITS MANY OTHER INCOMPARABLY OUTSTANDING
  FEATURES;
ITS COMPLETE PERFECTION.

Let us note these items briefly. First the testimony of the church. As we said above, the church lends no authority to the Bible. Only God does. At the same time, it is a very impressive fact that the church through the ages, in virtually all of its branches, has borne testimony to the Bible as the word of God. Of course, we do not go so far as Roman Catholics to claim that the testimony of the church itself proves the Bible to be the word of God, but the testimony of the church to the value of the Bible does indeed impress any detached and objective observer. It is quite notable that this book enjoys that distinction of so much prestigious endorsement for so many centuries. This continuing endorsement certainly calls attention to the significance of the Book, even if it does not prove the inspiration of it.

Second, Scripture itself refers more than three-thousand times to its inspiration. This is so impressive that many Christians rest their case for the inspiration of the Bible on that testimonial of the Bible to itself. This is probably not rationally justifiable. Even if the Bible said three million times that it was the word of God, that would not itself alone prove the Bible to be the word of God. But we may say surely that if the Bible did not claim to be the word of God, it certainly would not qualify. It is impressive that this book, especially this book, makes such an eminent claim. It may not prove what it claims to be by its mere claim, but it certainly is impressive that a book which has so many extraordinary qualities does indeed claim to be no mere human document.

Third is ITS SPIRITUAL SUBJECT MATTER. One has only to read the Babylonian epic of Gilgamesh about the creation and compare it with the opening chapters of Genesis to see what the *Westminster Confession* means by its SPIRITUAL SUB- JECT MATTER. The Bible not only deals with such a mundane matter as the creation in a sublime and spiritual manner but is quite obviously spiritual when it is discussing such a redemp- tive theme as man's salvation after the fall. Its spirituality is quite evident when one thinks of the 23rd Psalm, Amos's mighty declaration about war and peace, I Corinthians 13, or John 3:16. We know what the framers of this creed had in mind by the evidence that Scripture provides for its own inspiration in the very nature of its content. The Golden Rule (Matthew 7.12) is a kind of indication that this is a Golden Book.

Fourth is THE EFFECTIVENESS OF ITS TEACHING. James Russell Lowell has written somewhere: "show me a place on the face of the earth ten miles square where a man may provide for his children in decency and comfort, where age is venerated, where womanhood is protected, where human life is held in due regard, and I will show you a place where the gospel of Jesus Christ has gone before and laid the founda- tion." That gospel, of course, comes from this book and the power of its doctrine has been demonstrated repeatedly in the history of Christian expansion throughout the world. What other book being dropped in the midst of a degenerate and pagan culture has been able to transform the lives of in- dividuals and the society in which they live? Of course, we learn from the Scriptures themselves that it is not, strictly speaking, the effectiveness of its teaching but rather the fact that the Holy Spirit accompanies its teaching and makes the teaching effec- tive. The Holy Spirit (not marching armies) accompanies this book to energize it and make it powerful to the destroying of the strongholds of evil and the establishment of holiness in the hearts of men.

Let us leave as obvious the meaning of the reference to the MAJESTY OF ITS STYLE in the fifth item and comment more particularly on the sixth—AGREEMENT OF ALL ITS PARTS. When you realize that we are dealing with sixty-six different books written by some forty different authors over a period of about fifteen-hundred years, the agreement of all its parts is a phenomenal fact indeed. Each of us has personally written a number of books. Although their number is considerably less than sixty-six, we would still be completely amazed if each of our works agrees in all its parts.

There are some contemporary writers who see different theologies in the Bible. We believe, however, that they are "seeing things." What they think are differing theologies are simply differing aspects of the same theology. For example, some think that the strong predestinarianism is in conflict with the invitations of the Bible which put a premium on genuine free choices of man. But no one has ever shown that the sovereignty of God does indeed violate the free will of his creatures. No one has ever demonstrated that these two are conflicting ideas. There seems to be no reason at all why God cannot sovereignly carry out His will with consenting human agents who are not at all forced to make choices which they are not inclined to make. On the contrary, the agreement of the parts of the Bible is quite evident in such teachings, which do justice at once to the indisputable sovereignty of God and the equally indisputable freedom of man. Nowhere does the Bible deny the sovereignty of God or deny the free choices of man. On the contrary, it affirms throughout both of these and thereby indicates that they are not in any disharmony with each other. Judging from the frequency with which people gratuitously attribute conflict between them, the Bible is all the more impressive in affirming both and inferring the harmony between each.

To take one other important example, the Bible affirms the grace of God and at the same time the responsibility of men to do good works. People are often tempted to think that, if salvation is by grace, human endeavor is nullified. On the other hand, if emphasis is placed on human responsibility, that excludes the possibility of grace. The Bible, however, presents as its central message a grace which enables men to endeavor after nothing less than moral perfection. We have a remarkable agreement of its teachings in areas where, at first glance, we might suppose discrepancy.

Seventh, the *Confession* mentions the Bible's UNIFIED AIM FROM BEGINNING TO END (TO GIVE ALL GLORY TO GOD). Considering that the Bible was written by men and obviously for the interests of men, it is all the more remarkable that it keeps its eye single on the glory of God. Man's fall and redemption are the centers of its interest, but it never loses sight of the purpose of the fall, judgment, and redemption revealing the glory of God.

The eighth consideration may well be the most impressive of all: THE FULL REVELATION IT MAKES OF THE ONLY WAY OF MAN'S SALVATION. Not only does the Bible claim to present in its central figure, Jesus Christ, the way, the truth, and the life, but it demonstrates that the way of eternal life in Christ is the only way of man's salvation. When we speak about salvation of sinners by a Holy God, we have two facts to keep constantly in focus. First is that God, being holy, cannot possibly condone sin. On the other hand, man, being sinful, cannot possibly provide a holiness acceptable to God. How is this dilemma to be overcome except by God's holiness somehow coming in a way that makes the sinner acceptable to God? Obviously that is the only possible way of salvation. Equally obviously, the Bible depicts that only way of salvation. No other book has ever even imagined it.

The writers of the *Confession,* apparently aware that they could use all the rest of their thirty-three chapters merely describing the features of the Bible, decided to round off this discussion with some comprehensive terms. Thus we come to the concluding expressions. Ninth is ITS MANY OTHER IN-COMPARABLY OUTSTANDING FEATURES, and tenth ITS COMPLETE PERFECTION. You name it, the Bible has it.

All of these perfections are those by which the SCRIPTURE ITSELF SHOWS IN SO MANY WAYS THAT IT IS GOD'S WORD. SHOWS means demonstrates or proves that the Bible is the word of God. In the original *Westminster Confession* the word is "evidence." That word "evidence" is more clearly indicative of proof. Nevertheless, the word SHOWS is an acceptable contempory synonym. The meaning is unmistakable. This combination of excellences demonstrates, shows, evidences, proves the Bible to be what it indeed says it is and what the church has always affirmed it to be, namely, THE WORD OF GOD. In other words, we are not taking the doctrine of inspiration on mere faith. Rather the *evidence* is that the Bible is the word of God. It is calling for faith to be sure. But faith based on evidence. It is not calling for blind faith. It is not asking the believer in inspiration for a crucifixion of the intellect. On the contrary, it is asking persons to act intelligently, to respond to the evidence with faith in what the evidence demonstrates. This book is in fact nothing less or other than the word of God.

That being the case, we may be surprised to see that the *Confession* does not claim persuasive power for the Bible. Even though these excellences prove the Bible is the word of God, the *Confession* says that no one will be persuaded by that proof. As a matter of fact, something else has to be added, not to *prove* the Bible is the word of God but to *persuade* the reader to accept that proof. HOWEVER, WE ARE COMPLETELY PERSUADED AND ASSURED OF THE INFALLIBLE TRUTH AND DIVINE AUTHORITY OF THE BIBLE ONLY BY THE INWARD WORKING OF THE HOLY SPIRIT, WHO TESTIFIES BY AND WITH THE WORD IN OUR HEARTS.

Once again, one wonders why, if the Bible has such compelling evidence, it does not compel the reader to accept what it proves. The explanation will be given later in Chapter 6, which deals with the fall of man and sin. Man is a sinner, the *Confession* is going to tell us. The reason a sinful man reading the Bible and being confronted with this overpowering evidence does not assent to it is not because the evidence is not overpowering but because a sinner is unwilling to admit it.

You ask why a sinner is unwilling to admit the truth of Holy Scripture, the center of which is the gospel of divine grace? That is a good question. One would suppose that the sinner would be most willing to accept the good news that he can have his sins pardoned. One would not expect anything more than the goodness of the news being necessary to persuade him to accept it. Why does he refuse it and reject it and need the persuasion of the Spirit before he will ever come to believe it? The answer is that, though man is a sinner, he does not admit it. Being a sinner, he loves sin. He is not about to part with it.

So there is a double jeopardy in this good news. On the one hand, one is told by the Bible that he is a sinner. He does not want to admit that. If he does not accept this good news to turn to Jesus, who will save him from his sins? Yet he does not want to be saved *from* his sins. He wants to be saved *in* his sins. He loves his sins. He does not want to part with them. The gospel requires just that. That turns good news into bad news.

Enter the persuader, the Holy Spirit. He is the one WHO TESTIFIES BY AND WITH THE WORD IN OUR HEARTS. He accompanies the word of God with all its evidences. Working in our hearts, He inclines us toward virtue and away from sin, toward truth and away from error, toward Christ and away from unbelief. This persuasion of the Holy Spirit is not by adding more evidence. That is quite unnecessary. He changes the heart. This is absolutely necessary.

1.6 Section 6 shows the sufficiency and, yes, the insufficiency of Scripture. There is a sense in which the Scripture is insufficient. The *Confession* points that out before the paragraph is over. However, the emphasis of the section concerns not the limitations of the Bible but its glorious adequacy. EVERYTHING PERTAINING TO HIS OWN GLORY AND TO MAN'S SALVATION, FAITH, AND LIFE IS EITHER EXPLICITLY STATED IN THE BIBLE OR MAY BE DEDUCED AS INEVITABLY AND LOGICALLY FOLLOWING FROM IT. We have already seen that this book tells us the only way of salvation. Now we are told that this book tells us everything that is necessary to know about salvation. Everything necessary to be known for the salvation of our eternal souls is either stated expressly or implicitly in the Scripture. Two centuries earlier in Britain John Wycliffe had said the same thing. The Bible is the word of God *explicite* and *implicite*. Whatever the Bible expressly states is the word of God leading to our salvation. But the Bible can state truths implicitly as well as expressly. This passage is saying that when the Bible teaches anything by implication it is teaching that truth as well as when it expresses it in so many words.

Many people have an uneasiness about implications and deductions. There is no need for this fear. Most of what the Bible teaches is implicit. We are always drawing *deductions* from it. When the Bible says that you, whoever you are, shall not kill, it also says that to us and everyone else. You, whoever you are, and we and everyone else shall not kill. To be sure, your name is not in the Bible, nor are ours, but when the Bible says, however, "thou shalt not kill," it is perfectly obvious that it applies to all mankind. Since we are men, it applies to us. It would not be at all clearer that we are forbidden to murder if our names were in the Book. Yet that is an implication. Neither does it say: "Douglas Kelly, Philip Rollinson, John Gerstner, believe on the Lord Jesus Christ and you shall be saved." Yet, that is exactly what it does say. It makes it perfectly clear that the only way of salvation for any human being anywhere at any time is by faith in Jesus Christ. Because we are human beings, sinners, in need of grace, we know full well that our name is on that invitation to believe on the Lord Jesus Christ and be saved. It would not be at all clearer if we read our names in the Bible pages.

NOTHING IS AT ANY TIME TO BE ADDED TO THE BIBLE, EITHER FROM NEW REVELATIONS OF THE SPIRIT OR FROM TRADITIONS OF MEN. Drawing implications which are unmistakably in the Bible is one thing. Adding meanings to the Bible is something else again. One is absolutely necessary to practice. The other is absolutely necessary to avoid. One is essential to salvation. The other actually brings damnation. You have often heard it said that people can get anything they want out of the Bible. It is true that they *can* but not legitimately.

If they want to force the Scripture to say something they want it to say, they *can* do that. But they cannot do so *legitimately.*

The *Confession* hastens to indicate that although we are strictly forbidden to add to or subtract from Scripture, nevertheless, WE DO RECOGNIZE THAT THE INWARD ILLUMINATION OF THE SPIRIT OF GOD IS NECESSARY FOR A SAVING UNDERSTANDING OF THE THINGS WHICH ARE REVEALED IN SCRIPTURE. Illumination is not revelation. Illumination or understanding of the revelation is no addition to it. It is only a penetration of it. True understanding of the Bible can only come by the Holy Spirit in His glorious work of illumination.

A little boy brought an orange to his teacher one day and said, "It has been squeezed some, but there is more in it yet." There is more in the Bible than the church has ever yet discovered. That more must not be added by men but brought out by the Holy Spirit. The New Testament church has been at this job under the guidance of the Spirit for two thousand years. Certainly we understand the Bible better now than when the canon was closed. The famous words of John Robinson, pastor of the Pilgrims, are absolutely correct: "There is more light yet to break forth from its pages." Robinson believed firmly in the closed canon. Nothing is to be added to the Scripture. When he talked about new light, he did not mean new light added to the Bible, but new light extracted from it.

The very last sentence of this section has reference to what we call the "insufficiency" of the Bible. WE ALSO RECOGNIZE THAT SOME PROVISIONS FOR THE WORSHIP OF GOD AND THE GOVERNMENT OF THE CHURCH ARE SIMILAR TO SECULAR ACTIVITIES AND ORGANIZATIONS; THESE ARE TO BE DIRECTED ACCORDING TO OUR *NATURAL UNDERSTANDING* AND OUR *CHRISTIAN DISCRETION* AND SHOULD CONFORM TO THE GENERAL RULES OF THE WORD WHICH ARE ALWAYS TO BE OBSERVED (our italics). The Bible tells us that we are to worship God on the Sabbath day. But the Bible does not tell us what hours. Is it to be 7 o'clock, 8 o'clock, 9 o'clock, 10 or 11? Should there be another service in the evening at 6 o'clock, 7 o'clock, 8 o'clock. How long should the service last? What are the precise parts of a proper worship of God on Sunday? These the *Confession* calls "secular" matters, even though they have to do with the worship of God. The church, following her common sense, is to determine in a given situation the best time to worship, the best way to proceed, etc.

Please notice that the last part of the sentence warns us that we do not have the right, even in these "secular" matters, to violate the GENERAL RULES OF THE WORD. Take the sabbath. Is it proper to start Sunday services on Saturday night? A number of people might prefer public worship on Saturday night rather than on Sunday morning. The Bible commands us to keep the Sabbath day holy. Our forebears believed that the sabbath day began at sunset, Saturday night, and concluded at sunset on Sunday night. Generally speaking, the church has believed that where you begin those twenty-four hours is almost a secular matter — Sunday morning to Monday morning or Saturday sunset to Sunday sunset. But, as we are presently in the United States operating on the principle that the Lord's day goes from Sunday morning to Monday morning or from Saturday midnight to Sunday midnight, it would not be consistent or proper to start the Sabbath day at a time which the church did not recognize as the Sabbath day and terminate it before the time which it recognizes as the end. In other words it may be an optional matter whether to go from sunset to sunset or morning to morning or midnight to midnight, but once one has selected the appropriate period, he does not have the option of violating that period. Since we are now committed to the twenty-four hour period of Saturday midnight to Sunday midnight, we cannot actually exempt our people from the observance of the Sabbath day by arbitrarily adding a Saturday night as a kind of substitute. According to the *Westminster Confession* then certain things have to be done according to our wise discretion but never at the expense of THE GENERAL RULES OF THE WORD.

1.7 This is a very consoling paragraph, especially the statement that every text of Scripture is NOT EQUALLY CLEAR TO EVERYONE. Many people find it difficult to understand the

Bible. Ministers have to admit, as well as lay people, that not every individual passage is clear to everyone of them either. Many passages of the Bible are unclear, at first reading, certainly. We appreciate recognition of this truth by the fine assortment of theologians who drew up this great confession.

Nevertheless, this consolation follows on the heels of the assertion that EVERYTHING WHICH WE HAVE TO KNOW, BELIEVE, AND OBSERVE IN ORDER TO BE SAVED IS SO CLEARLY PRESENTED AND REVEALED *SOMEWHERE* IN THE BIBLE THAT THE UNEDUCATED AS WELL AS THE EDUCATED CAN SUFFICIENTLY UNDERSTAND IT BY THE PROPER USE OF THE ORDINARY MEANS OF GRACE (our italics). A learned scientist once said, "never overestimate the knowledge of your audience but never underestimate its capacity for knowledge." This is precisely what the Westminster divines are saying here. Many lay people may lack understanding of some parts of Scripture, but they are quite capable of understanding it, if they will read the Bible as a whole. Ministers will, of course, make that even easier. We are assured that *anyone,* educated or uneducated, will be able to understand the essential message of salvation by reading the Bible as a whole.

1.8 Notice that the inspiration of the Holy Scripture is here tied to the original languages in which God gave the Bible. The Old Testament in Hebrew and the New Testament in Greek WERE DIRECTLY INSPIRED BY GOD. If God wrote this book, it, of course, has to be without error. If God DIRECTLY IN-SPIRED this book, it has to be without error. That applies to the original language in which God DIRECTLY INSPIRED the Bible. For this reason good seminaries require the study of Hebrew and Greek.

There is no such thing as being a satisfactory expositor of the word of God, if one does not have access to the original languages in which it was written. It is true of any literature that no translation is absolutely satisfactory. If one wants to be certain about the meaning of a passage, the original tongue is indispensable. A minister does not have to be a specialist in these languages, but he has to know them well enough to be able to read critical commentaries and investigate learned journals and pursue lexicons. These are the tools of his trade.

We can understand all that is essential to salvation without ever knowing a word of Hebrew or Greek. We do have many excellent translations. But it is essential for the minister, who must enter into difficult and controverted passages, to know the original languages. These are not necessary to salvation. Everything which God has revealed is important, however, and should be understood. As specialists in the word of God, the ministers are obliged, of course, to have that kind of professional expertise.

The term autographa is in wide current use among churchmen. Defenders of the classic doctrine of the inerrancy of Scripture always insist that inerrancy applies only to these original manuscripts, namely the autographa. Inerrantists do not claim infallibility or inspiration for the transmission of the text, for the translation of the text, for the interpretation of the text, or for the proclamation of the text. Inerrancy applies only to the original text to which we can approach very, very closely by the science of textual criticism.

What about this problem of transmission? If the transmission is not as infallible as the original inspiration of the autographa, how do we know that we have a reliable text as the basis for our particular translation into English? Our *Confession* addresses itself to this subject. These manuscripts HAVE BEEN KEPT UNCONTAMINATED THROUGHOUT TIME BY HIS SPECIAL CARE AND PROVIDENCE. THEY ARE THEREFORE AUTHENTIC AND ARE TO BE THE CHURCH'S ULTIMATE SOURCE OR APPEAL IN EVERY RELIGIOUS CONTROVERSY. In the original *Westminster Confession*, the word was not UNCONTAMINATED but "pure". Uncontaminated is not quite synonymous with pure. Admittedly, it is practically synonymous. To be pure, it would have to be uncontaminated. But, we probably use the word pure, and they probably used the word pure in the seventeenth century, a little less stringently than that. We know from the writing of the *Westminster Confession* that those who penned it did not believe that the transmission was absolutely perfect, free of any contamination or corruption of the text. The manuscripts have been kept remarkably pure. Considering the long period of time, it is amazing how pure the manuscripts are. Those who copied the manuscripts of the bible often did so, not word for word, but letter for letter.

Whatever little contamination has crept in, we are usually able by the science of textual criticism to detect and remove. The main word here is AUTHENTIC. We do not have the inerrant autographa. We do have, however, such a close approximation to them in the manuscripts that it could be said, even in the seventeenth century, that the text we have is AUTHENTIC.

The paragraph ends with a genuine concern for the non-professionals, the laymen. It recognizes that they do not usually have a knowledge of the original language. But, they must have and do have a RIGHT TO THE BIBLE. Therefore, the Bible is to be translated into their vernacular languages. As a result, EVERYONE WILL BE ABLE TO WORSHIP GOD IN AN AC-CEPTABLE WAY. This is even truer today than it was when those words were written. We have many more translations into the language of the people than they ever dreamed of at the time of the Westminster Assembly. These translations range from near paraphrases to meticulous, almost word-for-word, renderings. There is just about no shade of meaning of the original words which (through the help of various publica-tions) any layman cannot relatively easily understand. Our main problem today is that there are so many excellent trans-lations that lay men and women may have difficulty determin-ing which one mainly to use.

From time to time, unfortunately, there are some who have been inclined to take away from the people this glorious privilege of excellent translations. There was one preacher, for example, who insisted that his people sing the Psalms in the original Hebrew. He himself would preach from the original text and expected his congregation to know the meaning of those foreign words. His zeal for the inerrant Scriptures and for his people knowing the pure word of God was highly admirable.

His judgment was not so commendable. Granted that it would be better if everybody mastered Hebrew and Greek and could read the text easily and knowledgeably in the original tongues. That is, however, absolutely out of the realm of feasibility. We can rejoice that God has provided us with so many excellent, easily accessible versions of Holy Scripture.

1.9 Here again we have a clear affirmation of the Reformation position on Biblical authority in sharp contrast to that of the Roman Catholic church, which taught then, as it teaches now, that the church of Rome is appointed by God to be the interpreter of the Bible. The Bible cannot be understood accurately or with confidence and certainty apart from the official teaching of that denomination. The *Confession* says to the contrary that THE INFALLIBLE STANDARD FOR THE INTERPRETATION OF THE BIBLE IS THE *BIBLE ITSELF.* Sola Scriptura! By Scripture alone is Scripture to be understood. The church can help in understanding the Bible. The minister is a specialist who can aid the less trained parishioner. Nonetheless, the Bible is for all, can and must be understood by all. This is the famous doctrine of the perspicuity of Scripture--the see-throughability of Scripture.

The analogy of faith is also stated here. One passage of Scripture can explain another passage MORE PLAINLY. Augustine is famous for the statement: "In the Old Testament the New Testament is latent; in the New Testament the Old Testament is patent." He is saying about the two Testaments that what is hidden in the Old becomes plain in the New. The fundamental point is that the Bible is sufficient for the understanding of the Bible. The church is a help but not a necessity. People can find their own way through the Scriptures to the Savior. The Berean laymen were "more noble," because they searched the Scriptures for themselves (Acts 17.11).

1.10 Finally, as the grand conclusion to this grand chapter we have a magnificient statement about the authority of the Bible. We have heard about the *inspiration* of the Bible by the Spirit. We have heard about the *illumination* of the Bible by the

Spirit. Now we hear about the *enlivening* of the Bible by the Spirit. The Holy Spirit speaks and is speaking in the Bible. He not only *has spoken* when He inspired it. He *is speaking* in the Bible now.

What does that mean? It means that when you read and listen to the Bible, you are listening to nothing other than the very words of the Holy Spirit. If He actually appeared to you supernaturally and literally spoke to you conversationally, that would be nothing other than what He is doing every time you listen to the Bible. You are hearing nothing other than the word of the Spirit.

But, you say, the Spirit said that centuries ago. I could understand it, you say, if it said that these words you read in the Bible are what the Holy Spirit *once spoke*. What am I to make of the statement that the Holy Spirit is speaking in the Bible?

You are quite right. The Spirit is not repeating audibly or articulating what He once led men to write. The Westminster divines mean that the word which He once spoke, thousands of years ago, is still true. It is still His word. The Westminster theologians were no mystics. They did not mean for a moment that you are to close you eyes and fancy you are hearing with your ears the voice of the Spirit of God. No. They want your eyes open. They want you reading, pondering, meditating on, and understanding the word of God which the Spirit inspired. But they also want you to know that you are not only reading something which God *once* uttered. You are reading something which He is making alive as you read it now. It is just as truly His word as if He supernaturally appeared and spoke the same words to you. You in your soul recognize that you are having communion with the Holy Spirit as well as reading His words. He is, as it were, speaking audibly to you. They are still His words. He is saying them to *you* now, as He said then to the church once long ago.

In a certain sense this is mysticism. It is a mysticism in which the Westminster divines did believe. It was a mysticism *in* the word, not apart from it. The kind of mysticism these scholars opposed was that which taught that the Spirit continued to reveal Himself *apart from or in addition to* the Bible. In their opinion that was a pernicious notion. But with all their hearts they believed that the Spirit did commune with the devout reader *in* the word of God.

This last section continues by saying that THE HOLY SPIRIT SPEAKING IN THE BIBLE IS THE SUPREME JUDGE OF ALL RELIGIOUS CONTROVERSIES, ALL DECISIONS OF RELIGIOUS COUNCILS, ALL THE OPINIONS OF ANCIENT WRITERS, ALL HUMAN TEACHINGS, AND EVERY PRIVATE OPINION. The Bible is the sole criterion of truth. Every theologian, every controversy, every council has to be judged by the word of God. If they be not according to that, there is no light in them. The *Confession* is saying that and *more* than that. It is also saying that when we test the deliberations of the church down through the ages by the Scriptures, God is testing His church by His word. This is not a static conception of Scripture. The Bible is not a dead book, once for all completed and finished. It is once for all completed and finished, but the Spirit of God is not finished with it. He is continuing to use it. He is literally speaking by it. He is adding nothing to it. He is allowing us to subtract nothing from it. But He is as vitally concerned in it now as when He first inspired it.

There is a difference here. When we read it and interpret it and expound its meaning, we are not inspired as the original writers were inspired when they recorded the original speaking of the Holy Spirit. Nevertheless, although we are uninspired as we deliberate on the words of Scripture, the Holy Spirit is speaking to us. While His message can be to a degree contaminated by our corruptions, He is nonetheless still speaking and still heard. We must be aware of our corruption and ride herd on it. We must be very judgmental about ourselves in order more clearly to hear the pure speech of the Spirit in the word.

This puts an entirely different light on the historic controversies and the councils of the church. The Spirit has been speaking through His word through the centuries. At the same time human corruption has also been active. How are we to determine what is the speech of the inerrant Spirit and what is the speech of errant man? By the word of God. By listening carefully to it. By subjecting our own tendency to pervert it. By our willingness to be in conformity to it.

The *Confession* concludes this section with the assertion that WE ARE TO BE SATISFIED WITH THE JUDGMENT OF HIM WHO IS AND CAN BE THE ONLY JUDGE. Having done all in our power to compare Scripture with Scripture, to listen carefully to what it is saying, to criticize ruthlessly our own tendency to wrest Scripture, we can indeed approach the truth of the living God. We can be satisfied in our judgment with the judgment of Him Who is and can be the only judge. If we do our job properly, our judgment will be His judgment, and His judgment ours. We can rest then in our judgment, not because it is ours but because it is His. There can be no final court of appeal other than the Holy Spirit speaking in Holy Scripture.

It is appropriate to close with the immortal words of Martin Luther accounting for his actions before the Emperor Charles V in 1520.

> Unless I am convinced by the testimony of the Scriptures or by clear reason (for I do not trust either in the pope or in councils, since . . . they have often erred). I am bound by the Scriptures . . . and my conscience. I cannot do otherwise; here I stand; may God help me. Amen.

Luther was saying that unless he could hear the Spirit speaking in the Bible, he could not accept the verdict of that court or any church. He could only BE SATISFIED WITH THE JUDGMENT OF HIM WHO IS AND CAN BE THE ONLY JUDGE–THE HOLY SPIRIT SPEAKING IN THE BIBLE. That is the voice of faith responding to the voice of the Spirit of God.

Chapter 2

Concerning God and the Holy Trinity

The three sections of the second chapter deal first with God as He is with regard to His attributes, second as He is in relation to His creation, and third as He is within Himself.

2.1. This section deals with God as He is in Himself in His attributes, natural and moral, with the emphasis here on the natural. The *Confession* notices these natural attributes of God: unity, life, infinity, spirituality, unchangeability, immensity, eternality, incomprehensibility, omnipotence, omniscience, invisibility, immateriality, indivisibility, and impassibility.

Two of these attributes demand more attention. One is what is indicated above as God's "impassibility." The original *Confession* asserts that God is without "passions." The key proof text, cited in the *Confession*, is Acts 14.15, where Paul asserts to the citizens of Lystra that he and Barnabas are not gods (Paul has just healed a crippled man) but humans just like they are. Paul uses the expression, "we also are men of like passions with you" (KJV). The *Confession* follows the King James' literal translation of the Greek compound, *homoiopathēs,* using the English "passion" for the Greek root *pathos.* The general sense of the ancient Greek word *pathos* and the English word passion (in the seventeenth century and earlier) is what we now call emotions, and so the Summertown version renders "passions" here by HUMAN EMOTIONS. There is a narrower sense of both the ancient Greek word and seventeenth-century English "passion" meaning desires and particularly sexual desires. This narrower sense is how *pathos* is generally used in the New Testament (e.g. in Col 3.5 or 1 Thes 4.5). However, the compound adjective, *homoiopathēs*, never has that narrow sense and means "having like feelings or passions" (Liddell and Scott), referring to one "whose attitude or feeling is the same or similar" (Friedrich). And so Paul and the Westminster Assembly distinguish God from humans as having no human emotions (and similarly in Jas 5.17 in reference to Elijah as a mere human being, the only other use of the word *homoiopathēs* in the New Testament).

The problem here is that God is frequently described in the Bible as having some emotions at least which are analogous to human ones. Explaining this passage in the *Confession*, R. L. Dabney identifies these as "active principles" in God, which "must not be conceived of as emotions, in the sense of ebbing and flowing accesses of feeling."

> They lack that agitation and rush, that change from cold to hot, and hot to cold, which constitute the characteristics of passion in us. They are, in God, an ineffable, fixed, peaceful, unchangeable calm, although the springs of volition. (*Lectures,* 153)

This issue is not a dead one, however, and theologians to this day are arguing about whether and if and how God does or does not have an "emotional" nature. There is even disagreement among the three of us. Gerstner believes that the scope of the *Confession's* reference here to the absense of "passions" in God is limited to His not having bodily feelings or sensations.

The second question about these natural attributes has to do with God's "incomprehensibility." The original text has "incomprehensible," for which the Summertown version renders BEYOND OUR UNDERSTANDING, meaning that He cannot be completely or exhaustively known or comprehended by human beings. But the *Confession* certainly does not mean here that God cannot be apprehended by the mind or known at all. He can be truly known but never exhaustively. He is hidden but not completely hidden.

The second list of God's moral attributes includes: holiness, freedom, absoluteness. The *Confession* probably uses holiness as a common or generic term for the sum of all virtues, since it does not mention love, kindness, joy, goodness, etc.

His moral qualities are crucial. Lacking them would make God great but not good. "How great Thou art" is not nearly so important as "How good Thou art." Our God is great and good, and only great because He is good.

Thirdly and finally the attributes of God are described in their operation or exercise: ACCORDING TO HIS OWN WILL, FOR HIS GLORY, LOVINGLY, graciously, mercifully, patiently, overflowingly, forgivingly, rewardingly, and inexorably — against sin and the guilty sinner. This description does bring many other moral virtues into view, some of which (e.g. love) are native to God whether or not there was a creation and some which (e.g mercy) imply or assume the misery of the creature.

2.2 This section deals with God as He is in relation to His creation. It has already been implied in the first section that God is independent. Here it is stated explicitly that He has everything IN AND OF HIMSELF. Obviously if God is ALL-SUFFICIENT, He does not NEED ANY OF HIS CREATION, DERIVE ANY GLORY FROM THEM, but on the contrary MANIFESTS HIS OWN GLORY IN, BY, UNTO, AND ON THEM (because He is their only SOURCE ON WHOM THEIR VERY EXISTENCE DEPENDS). From this it clearly follows that HE HAS COMPLETELY SOVEREIGN DOMINION over them and does WHATEVER HE PLEASES with them. Should it be asked whether God meets the job-description for running the universe, the answer is that HIS KNOWLEDGE IS INFINITE, INFALLIBLE, and independent, so that nothing is CONDITIONAL (or uncertain, in the sense of dependent on anything not under God's control).

With all that, all that power and wisdom, can God be trusted? Certainly, because HE IS COMPLETELY HOLY IN ALL HIS PURPOSES, WORKS, AND COMMANDS. Consequently we creatures not only carry out His will but owe Him WORSHIP, SERVICE, OR OBEDIENCE.

2.3 This third section treats God's triune being within Himself. In the unity of God there is also diversity, THREE PERSONS. But this diversity does not destroy the unity of ONE SUB-

STANCE, POWER, AND ETERNITY. The three persons in unity are GOD THE FATHER, GOD THE SON, AND GOD THE HOLY SPIRIT. In the trinity the Father EXISTS, He is, the Son is GENERATED, and the Spirit PROCEEDS. (Note that the Father's existence does not imply that the other two persons did not at one time exist, since, as the first sentence of this section points out, all three persons are coeternal.) The Son is, however, from the Father eternally, and the Spirit from the Father and the Son eternally.

There is a very significant difference in the understanding and description of the trinity between eastern (Greek Orthodox, Russian Orthodox, and other churches coming from the Eastern Roman Church based in Constantinople) and western Christendom — the famous *filioque* [literally "and from the Son"] controversy. The western churches maintain that the Spirit proceeds FROM THE FATHER AND THE SON (*filioque*), while Eastern Orthodoxy denies it. Western Christology, including especially John Calvin, has repudiated any natural subordination of the Son to the Father. The Son is absolutely equal to the Father, and the Holy Spirit is absolutely equal with both.

Even within the Eastern Orthodox tradition, however, one line of classical theologians (for example, Athanasius, Gregory Nazianzus, and Epiphanius) has strongly affirmed the full equality of the Son and Spirit with the Father. While these theologians do not specifically affirm *filioque*, they do join with the West in denying subordination of the second and third persons of the Trinity.

Chapter 3

Concerning God's Eternal Decrees

This famous chapter on God's eternal decrees makes eight statements in the form of four couplets. First, God has foreordained everything that happens, but, second, not on the basis of foreknowledge. Third, for His glory He has predestined some people to life and foreordained others to death, and fourth, the precise numbers are fixed. Fifth, although these decrees are "unconditional," that does not (sixth) preclude MEANS. Seventh, these decrees include the passing by of some; but, eighth, this knowledge is expressed very carefully and is to be understood not only for the benefit of the elects' assured but also DILIGENT LIFE.

3.1 This section teaches that God's foreordination is total but that foreordination does not force the will of creatures. Let us note first of all that God has eternally ordained everything that happens in time. This ordination agrees with the previously reviewed natural attributes of God, His eternality, wisdom, and unchangeability, motivated by His moral (HOLY) and free (OWN) will. As long as God has been, the world has been on His mind, and His mind has been made up—freely not necessarily—morally not fatalistically—and unalterably not tentatively.

Absolute as these decrees are, they do *not* mean: that God is the author of sin, that man's will is forced, or that second causes are not real. Sin is ordained by God insofar as it is a large part of WHATEVER HAPPENS. But the *Confession* does not confuse ordaining and decreeing with authoring or producing. Here the distinction is drawn, which in later sections will be explained. Although ordaining everything that happens certainly includes the wills of men, God does not REPRESS, force, coerce, or do any violence to human wills. Mysterious as this may seem, there is no mystery about it being the teaching of the *Westminster Confession*. Man's FREEDOM is as clearly asserted as God's decrees. Second causes (God's will as cause being primary, first, or original) are real. God's decrees make them real or ESTABLISHED. Not only does He not obliterate human choices, rather His decrees actually establish or make those choices to exist along with all other SECONDARY CAUSES or means by which God brings about whatever He has ordained.

3.2 Although God foresees everything, His decrees are *not* mere ratification of what He sees will happen anyway. The *Confession* does not say here that God's foreknowledge depends on His decrees. Here it says that His decrees do not depend on His foreknowledge. Two heretical notions are hereby denied and rejected. One is the philosophical notion that ideas may exist independently of God and limit divine behavior. The other is the theological doctrine that eternal decrees concerning men rest on the foreseen acts of men.

3.3 This is an awesome paragraph. We may first observe that God's decrees concerning life and death are TO MANIFEST HIS GLORY. In Somerset Maugham's *Razor's Edge* Larry is offended with God because He creates everything for HIS GLORY. If Larry (or Maugham) had understood that it was for the *creature's sake* that God made everything for HIS GLORY, Larry would not have taken offense as he and multitudes of others mistakenly do. In glorifying God and only in glorifying God does man live. And so God insists that all things glorify Him.

We should also note here that God predestines to life but foreordains to death. For the Westiminster divines reprobation (being FOREORDAINED TO EVERLASTING DEATH) is a permissive decree. Predestination (being PREDESTINED TO EVERLASTING LIFE) is a positive decree. This distinction is clarified in Chapter 6. Also, when God predestinates some to life and foreordains others to death, He is looking at man as fallen. So, from the whole mass of perishing people (*ex massa perditionis*), i.e. all humankind, God mercifully predestinates some to live and justly foreordains the rest to be left to perish in their hell-deserving sins — i.e. He permits or allows them to remain in their lost condition. In this respect and historically speaking, the *Westminster Confession* is Augustinian and sublapsarian or infralapsarian (meaning that God eternally contemplated man, not as created [supralapsarian] but as fallen — see the excellent chart of the different views in Warfield's *Plan of Salvation*, p. 23).

3.4 The number of foreordained and predestinated is CERTAIN, DEFINITE, AND unchangeable. The point here is that *foreordination* to death or reprobation is as explicit as *predestination* to life or election. A local pastor once prayed for a visiting preacher that as a result of the message more souls would be added to the Lamb's Book of Life. He did not understand or believe this section of the *Confession*, that the number of elect in the Lamb's Book of Life has been precisely determined by God and is UNALTERABLE. The purpose of preaching is to gather out of the world that DEFINITE AND UNALTERABLE number. Paul endured all things for the elect's sake (2 Tm 2.10).

3.5 Section 5 contains the purest expression of God's unconditional election, which is ETERNAL, UNCHANGEABLE, and unknown (HIDDEN). Election is unknown to the elect for one very good reason: they do not then exist. Nor do they know it, when they are born, but only when or after they are born again. From all eternity God has had it in His heart to share His glory with some men and angels — for their sake, not His, but for His glory, not theirs. This election furthermore comes solely from God's mercy, love, and grace — not as a result of any deficiency (or necessity) in God any more than from any sufficiency (or merit) in man. Finally, election is INDEPENDENT of God's foreknowledge of the predestinated's faith or good works. Election then is independent of but not unrelated to faith and good works. We have already seen that God's decrees ESTABLISHED SECONDARY CAUSES (3.1), which are dependent on decrees, not decrees on them. In the next section the MEANS will be itemized.

3.6 This section points out that God has not only predestinated the end (i.e. salvation) but also the means. The elect are fallen in Adam, but they are redeemed by being EFFECTUALLY CALLED, JUSTIFIED, ADOPTED, SANCTIFIED, and KEPT. None but the elect receive these "means" of salvation. It seemed to the Westminster theologians that God would not take the means to save those He had not chosen to save. Neither this section nor this chapter, however, ends the treatment of this subject. GOD'S ETERNAL DECREES, as described in this chapter, do not produce fatalism and inactivity. Thirty more Westminster chapters follow, and they follow not only *on* but *from* the third.

3.7 Being sovereign in His mercy, God chose NOT TO CALL (savingly) THE REST OF MANKIND but TO ORDAIN THEM to the wrath due their sins in order to show HIS GLORIOUS JUSTICE. Here is expressly and unambiguously stated the doctrine of reprobation as Westminster finds it in the Bible. In its opinion Scripture teaches *election* and *reprobation* both *explicitly* and *implicitly.* This is an awesome doctrine, which the *Confession* does not shrink from articulating, as part of "the whole counsel of God" (Acts 20.27). We need to remember, of course, that all of the positions in the *Confession* are based on Scriptural texts. (The Assembly used: Mt 11.25,26; 1 Pt 2.8; Rom 9.17,18,21-22; Jude 4; 2 Tm 2.19,20; Rom 9.20, 11.33; Dt 29.29; 2 Pt 1.10; Eph 1.6; Rom 11.5,6,20; Rom 8.33; and Lk 10.20.   See notes 24-27 to Chapter 3 in the Summertown version of the *Confession,* which indicate the entire history of the proof texts from the original 1647 edition through the American Presbyterian additions and deletions.)

3.8 This MYSTERIOUS DOCTRINE is to be treated in such a way that those who are called may have an assurance of their eternal election and be moved to the praise of God and a DILIGENT LIFE. The awesome nature of reprobation does not divert attention from the fact that election is fundamentally an extremely comforting doctrine. Its being MYSTERIOUS does not mean that this doctrine is totally incomprehensible. However, great DISCRETION and care are necessary in treating it. It is not, as this section points out, simply by hearing this doctrine that assurance comes of being ETERNALLY CHOSEN but by obedience (OBEYING THE WILL OF GOD) — so that *you* may "make your . . . election sure" (1 Pt 1.10). In this context then election produces in the elect humility and a DILIGENT LIFE, which is what makes election sure to the elect.

Chapter 4

Concerning Creation

This chapter especially concentrates on two things: that God made everything out of nothing and that He made man in His own image.

4.1 The first section briefly reviews the *when* (IN THE BEGINNING), the *who* (GOD THE FATHER, SON, AND HOLY SPIRIT), the *how* (OUT OF NOTHING), the *what* (EVERYTHING), and the *why* (TO REVEAL THE GLORY OF HIS ETERNAL POWER, WISDOM, AND GOODNESS) of the six-day creation.

The expression IN THE BEGINNING (originating, of course, in the Biblical texts of Gen 1.1 and John 1.1) not only times the creation but times time itself, because before the creation there was no time. So, if the question is asked, when the creation occurred, the answer is when there was first a "when."

In the Old Testament God the Creator is plural (Elohim). This latent teaching is made explicit and patent in the trinitarian passages of the New Testament (e.g. Mt 28.19). Of God's power, the Westminster Assembly believed that the creation was *ex nihilo* (out of nothing), while being fully aware that *ex nihilo nihil fit* (out of nothing, nothing comes). For them God is the one and only Magician who really can bring a rabbit out of an empty hat. Again the *Confession* affirms that the creation was not for the Creator but for the creation itself, since its purpose was to reveal His glory, which He did not need to reveal to Himself.

4.2 This paragraph makes eight points about the creation of man. As created man was: male and female; rational; immmortal (in soul); endowed with knowledge, righteousness, and true holiness—the image of God; morally able to obey or disobey God; at liberty to do as the will chose; under law (internal, WRITTEN IN THEIR HEARTS, and external, NOT TO EAT FROM THE TREE OF THE KNOWLEDGE OF GOOD AND EVIL); and HAPPY (IN FELLOWSHIP WITH GOD and with DOMINION OVER THE OTHER CREATURES).

The identity of male and female in the original creation is recognized here as not being inconsistent with the differentiation between them (as in Gen 1.27). Man's rationality is also affirmed as a Biblical reality not merely a subsequent Greek philosophical notion. The basis of man's creation in the image of God is not an empty rational capability per se but rather a specific content with which man's personness and personality were endowed and imbued. This endowment was both natural (KNOWLEDGE) and moral (RIGHTEOUSNESS and TRUE HOLINESS). In Chapter 6 it will appear that the natural survives the fall but that the moral is destroyed by it.

Man's original, prelapsarian moral ability was to sin or not sin (*posse peccare aut posse non peccare*), but after the fall his moral ability became the ability only to sin. Original man had not only the ability to choose to obey or disobey but also the liberty to act. After the fall he lost the moral ability to obey, while preserving the natural ability to act. The underlying basis of this action, the internal law of the conscience, is permanent. The external, positive law, in this first case concerning the Tree, is impermanent, but it does test the internal and the permanent.

The basis of pre-fallen man's happiness was relational and two-fold. It consisted of FELLOWSHIP with God above man and DOMINION over creatures below man.

Chapter 5

Concerning Providence

In this chapter we find that God's providence maintains everything according to His will and for His glory by means of second causes, which may be ordinary or miraculous and which include a moral ordering of sin—extending even to the sins of His own people, although the sins of the wicked bring judgment on themselves, while all things (even sins) work together for good for God's church, His people.

5.1 Herein is the general statement about God's providence, that He maintains everything according to His will and for His glory. There are no loose ends in God's providence, which is completely comprehensive—extending to things (foreordination) and actions (predestination). Not a sparrow falls without God. The source of this providential control is completely free. God's will is utterly unconstrained and unlimited. However, His will is not according to whim but rather perfect foreknowledge. The goal or end of this divine providence is the glorification of God's WISDOM, POWER, JUSTICE, GOODNESS, AND MERCY. Again we see a division into two sets of divine attributes: the natural (WISDOM and POWER) and the moral (JUSTICE, GOODNESS, AND MERCY).

5.2 The first or primary cause of everything is God. He is the ultimate power which brings all things to pass. He could, presumably, effect everything by and of Himself alone without using intermediary causes. But the *Confession* teaches here that it pleases God to use means outside Himself, second causes, to accomplish many things. All things are UNCHANGEABLY AND INFALLIBLY determined by God's decree, but they "fall out" according to *their nature* as second causes. Of these second causes some are "necessary" — as an apple falls when dropped. Others are "free" — as a man *may* choose to drop the apple — or contingent — as the apple's falling *depends* on the choosing of the man holding it.

5.3 These second causes may be ordinary or extraordinary (i.e. miraculous). Ordinarily God uses ORDINARY MEANS. Bodies ordinarily sink below water. However, dispensing with second causes, e.g. gravitation, God may WORK WITHOUT, BEYOND, OR CONTRARY TO THESE (ORDINARY) MEANS, e.g. in directly causing Christ to walk on water. This kind of WORK is WITHOUT second causes, BEYOND the power of second causes, and CONTRARY to the natural tendencies of second causes. We see then that second causes may be CONTRARY to their natural tendency but never contrary to the first cause. The purpose of these extraordinary means is explained in the next section.

5.4 This section focuses on how sin is related to God's providence, which includes a moral ordering of sin. First of all this providential ordering of sin is positive and not merely permissive. The *Confession* does not exclude sin from God's providence, but neither does it allow Him to be the author of sin. Evil is neither the result of God's inability to prevent it nor of His production of it. These two fixed points of Reformed theology are clearly stated here.

Exactly how God accomplishes this is not stated, but this control applies not just to the continuation of sin in the course of world history but to the origin of human sin in the fall of Adam as well. The implications are also clear. Sinfulness DOES NOT PROCEED FROM GOD but BELONGS TO THE CREATURE, and so providential sins proceed from man. Therefore, God must provide the circumstances ORDERED by Him which become the occasion for the sinfulness of the predestined acts. Everything in this process is GOVERNED by Him.

God's purposes and the sinful creature's purposes in the same predestined sins of providence are exactly opposite.

God brings them about for holy purposes, the fallen creatures for sinful ones. An explicit illustration is found in one of the proof texts cited (Gn 37.18ff). God ordained the wicked selling of Joseph into slavery for the later redemption of the children of Israel, while Joseph's brothers did the wicked deed because of the their envious and hateful hearts.

5.5 This providential control extends even to the moral ordering of the sins of His own people. God does allow His people to be tempted and to sin. It is very important to note here that God *allows* but does not *permit* believers (the saved, His people) to sin. God never permits sin in the sense of making sin *morally* allowable. Whenever God permits sin, He does so only in the sense that He makes it psychologically possible.

We learn in this treatment as well that those who have become God's children are not so perfectly His children that they are incapable of any sin (as they will be in heaven). This point will be elaborated in the chapters that follow. If Christians wonder why God takes them the long wilderness-way to the heavenly land of promise, the *Confession* gives five reasons: to chastise them for their sins, to reveal the power of remaining sinfulness, to humble them, to make them more dependent on God, to alert them against future OPPORTUNITIES TO SIN. The discipline of God's sinning children here is not a condemning but a chastening. It may be in hot displeasure, but it is a loving Father's hot displeasure.

5.6 This section turns to those who are reprobated. Their sins bring judgment on them, because it is not as a Father but as THE RIGHTEOUS JUDGE that God hardens them IN THEIR OWN SINFULNESS. Four processes are involved. First of all God withholds saving grace from them (always). Secondly, He withdraws common grace (sometimes). Thirdly, He exposes the wicked to opportunities to sin, and finally He gives them over to the world, the flesh, and the devil. The result of these processes is that the reprobate HARDEN THEMSELVES EVEN UNDER THOSE CIRCUMSTANCES WHICH GOD USES TO SOFTEN OTHERS. Note that the saved and the reprobated are responding essentially to the same CIRCUMSTANCES differently — showing that it is the persons and not the circumstances which determine praiseworthy or blameworthy behavior. By their own doing believers make all circumstances blessings, while sinners make all circumstances cursings.

5.7 This short paragraph asserts that all things work together for good for God's church. The teaching of Section 6, that all providential circumstances tend to SOFTEN or bless God's children, is further developed here. Providential circumstances bless God's children intentionally IN A VERY SPECIAL WAY. In a general way God allows His providence to bring judgment on the wicked, but in a more positive SPECIAL WAY He designs the same providence to bless His people.

Chapter 6

Concerning the Fall of Man, Sin, and the Punishment for Sin

This chapter teaches us: how man sinned, why God permitted sin, and what the consequences of sin are for man and his progeny. ORIGINAL sin produces ACTUAL sins, and together they bring wrath, misery, and death—temporal and eternal.

6.1 Here two instruments in the origin of man's sin are noted: the seduction of Satan and the permission of God. The *Confession* states only the bare facts of the fall. It does not even state the problem, much less offer any solution. How a good man could incline to evil does not seem to have troubled the Assembly. Only the sheer Biblical account is offered. This avoidance may have been the best course, since every effort at explanation from Augustine to Jonathan Edwards has notoriously failed. The *Confession* simply cites the truth of the inspired Scripture. Whether they could (or we can) understand that truth or not neither adds to nor subtracts from its verity.

The fall could not have happened without God's permission, and it did not happen without Satan's temptation. God permits Satan to aim at his own glory in order to achieve God's glory. The smartest of the smart alecks seems never to realize that he is being "had."

6.2 The results of the fall involve both loss and gain. Loss of righteousness and communion, and gain of death and defilement. This tragic loss and horrendous gain were both the results of what the *Shorter Catechism* (Q. 14) and this very chapter (6.6) call "transgression" [or 'disobeying'] of the law. This disobeying of the law immediately involved privation of the good: THEY FELL FROM their goodness. Our original parents lost their ORIGINAL RIGHTEOUSNESS. Augustine's famous definition of evil as the absence of good seems to be implicit here. This loss spelled death. To live apart from God is death (1 Tm 5.6). Biblical and spiritual death is not the opposite of life but of virtue.

The resulting condition is "total depravity." Adam and Eve became COMPLETELY POLLUTED IN ALL THEIR FACULTIES AND PARTS OF BODY AND SOUL. This pollution *extends* to all parts of human nature.

6.3 This paragraph points out that *all* natural offspring have the sin of their first parents reckoned to them because Adam was the ROOT of the human family. This statement sounds very much like *mediate* imputation, a minority Reformed view held by Augustine and Calvin, which asserts that since all mankind derives from its first parents, by that same natural, organic derivation all mankind also derive their parents' pollusion and therefore guilt. *Immediate* imputation on the other hand questions the justice of holding descendants responsible for any ancestors' behavior merely because of their organic derivation without any direct moral involvement. The "federal" or representative view is adopted by the *Confession*, and for this it is historically famous. The federal view overcomes the apparent injustice of *mediate* imputation in seeing Adam in the divinely appointed role as *representatively* acting for his natural progeny. Can anyone question the right and fairness of God so to appoint, and, being more than fairly represented, is man not also fairly held responsible?

6.4 Because of this corruption into which man fell, human beings are totally disinclined—and therefore disabled and opposite to—all good and totally inclined to and practicing all sin. Here is a classic definition of total depravity. Man lacks all virtue and possesses all vice. Being disinclined totally to virtue, we are totally inclined to vice. Man is evil, nothing but evil, altogether evil, all the time. Man's heart is a seed bed of iniquity and hence always produces only wild fruit.

6.5 One does not escape this sin or its sinfulness entirely by regeneration, although the saved are PARDONED AND DEADENED through Christ. In Roman Catholic theology it is contended that the sin remaining after regeneration ("concupiscence") is not sinful. The *Confession* does not agree. Nevertheless, the sin remaining after regeneration is PARDONED by Christ. The question naturally arises how something can be sinful which is pardoned. The answer is that the pardon of Christ is applied to that sin *as, but not before, it occurs*. Not only are the acts sins but also the "impulse" to the acts, and both are pardoned. They are also DEADENED. "Crucified" is one Biblical term which means that the power of the "impulse" is dealt a fatal blow in regeneration — but is not totally destroyed. Professor John Murray used to say, "sin remains, but it does not reign."

6.6 Here we find that every sin (not just some) is mortal or deadly in its very nature, so that the unpardoned sinner is subjected to: THE WRATH OF GOD, THE CURSE OF THE LAW, and misery and DEATH (spritual, temporal, and eternal). God is in his heaven, as the poet says, but all is *not* well with the world. The Bible teaches the law of karma and actually more profoundly than do the Eastern religions. The CURSE OF THE LAW is that whatever a man sows that shall he perfectly reap. The RESULTANT MISERIES are eternal as well as temporal. All this — and hell, too. So far from the only hell being in this world, compared with real hell, the worst in the world is heaven. For the sinner, the only heaven is in this world, no matter how wretched his existence in this world may be.

Chapter 7

Concerning God's Covenant with Man

This chapter teaches us that the separation between God and man could only be bridged by divine condescension (covenants). The first of these was the covenant of works, the second the covenant of grace. The covenant of grace is often called a testament because of the death of Christ, the testator of the covenant. The covenant of grace was the same in the Old Testament, although administered by sacrifices. In the New Testament it is administered by the word and sacraments with the grand result that THERE ARE NOT THEN TWO ESSENTIALLY DIFFERENT COVENANTS OF GRACE, BUT ONE AND THE SAME COVENANT UNDER DIFFERENT DISPENSATIONS.

7.1 The fundamental basis of covenant, as outlined in this first paragraph, is the infinite distance between God and man, which makes man incapable of deserving anything from God except by the latter's infinite condescension. It is odd that the principal objection to covenant theology is that it regards God and man as being on the same level, when in fact it is the infinite elevation of God above man that necessitates the covenant. There is no equivalence of parties or contributions initially involved — no *quid pro quo* as in human covenants. *Of himself* man does not have — and never had or ever could have — anything to offer worthy of divine notice. We stress "of himself," because, as will be seen, man is *given* something to offer of infinite value — a perfect *quid pro quo* — in the sacrifice of the mediator.

7.2 The covenant of works was an agreement with Adam that he would receive life for himself and posterity ON THE CONDITION OF PERFECT, PERSONAL OBEDIENCE. The *Confession* does not say that Adam would receive life on the *merit* of obedience but merely on the *condition* of obedience. Some scholars read merit into this statement, but a condition need not be meritorious. Indeed the first section shows that this condition cannot be meritorious, because the creature could never receive a "reward" without divine condescension. This condition is analagous to the non-meritorious condition of faith in the covenant of grace. Therefore we should note that the Covenant of Works itself is gracious. It is gracious of God to promise Adam life ON THE CONDITION OF PERFECT, PERSONAL OBEDIENCE. It was infinitely condescending.

7.3 By the fall man lost all possibility of life by the covenant of works, because he became incapable of perfect obedience. Some other way of salvation was now needed. Scripture indicates that God had prepared for this need even before the world was created. Christ is called "the Lamb slain from the foundation of the world" (Rev 13.8). This indicates that God's plan to save us through the substitutionary work of His Son (that is, by grace, *not* by what we do) was arranged for in God's purposes before creation and thus even before the fall of Adam.

In one sense, even the Covenant of Works (or Life) was gracious in that God kindly condescended to relate to those (humankind) infinitely beneath Him and generously to grant them massive blessing (eternal life) for very little on their part (simple obedience, which they were fully capable of carrying out). But in every sense the full Covenant of Grace excels the Covenant of Works in its gracious, non-meritorious basis, for in this arrangement God deals with us not as we deserve but as His Son — in our place — deserves. Jesus lives a holy life for us (thus meriting the reward of heaven), and He dies an atoning death for us (thus delivering us from the punishment of Hell).

At the same time, totally gracious though it is, the Covenant of Grace has its legal aspects. Christ fulfilled and thus magnified every requirement of the Law. Also, the Holy Spirit motivates every believer from his innermost being to love and keep the Law of God (Jer 31.31-34, Jn 15.10-17, 1 Jn 2.3-5).

God FREELY OFFERS SINNERS the Covenant of Grace, but He gives the Spirit, who makes them WILLING, only to those ORDAINED TO LIFE. This may seem to be inconsistent, since many sinners are not ordained to life and therefore are not WILLING to receive the gospel offer. The Westminster divines were aware, however, that, although all men are sinners, only those who admit it are "effectually called." Christ came to call not the righteous but sinners — that is, those who admit that they are not righteous but acknowledge that they are sinners — to repentance (Mk 2.17). So, in the proper sense of the word only the regenerate elect are effectually called or offered the gospel. The others, considering themselves "righteous," are insulted by such an offer. If anyone actually and truly accepts the offer, he must have been born again.

7.4 The Covenant of Grace is often called a testament, because by His death Christ purchased the EVERLASTING INHERITANCE provided in it. One can readily see that covenant or agreement is not synonymous with testament or will of inheritance. But the testament does explain how God "freely offers life and salvation through Jesus Christ." It was by His death that Christ purchased life for His people. So the New Covenant in His blood is the testament in His blood.

Here is also the explanation why God can "freely" offer without violating His inexorable justice. By His death, Christ paid the penalty of sin, and His testament showed forth God's righteousness in forgiving believers. It is free for *them,* because it was paid for by Christ (at an infinite price).

7.5 This and the following section show that there were two different administrations of the same Covenant of Grace. This paragraph explains the operation of the Covenant of Grace in the Old Testament, where it was ADMINISTERED BY PROMISES, PROPHECIES, SACRIFICES, CIRCUMCISION, THE PASCHAL LAMB, AND OTHER TYPES AND ORDINAN-

CES . . .. So the Covenant of Grace *was* administered in the Old Testament. It was in operation. It did not begin with the coming of the incarnate Jesus Christ. The believing Jews were saved by the same covenant which saves Christians today. There is no difference in the covenant, in the people of God, or in the salvation.

To be sure the Covenant of Grace in the Old Testament was effected differently. Its effectiveness resided in the fact that those ORDINANCES foreshadowed Christ. They preached Christ, just as the ordinances of the church do today. Whenever and wherever Christ is set forth, salvation may follow. Those ancient ordinances were SUFFICIENT AND EFFECTIVE in their time. By implication they are not sufficient and effective in this day, because they have taken new form in the New Testament. It is as much a sin to observe a day of atonement today as it was a duty, privilege, and means of grace in the Old Testament times. Then, as now, the reason for the efficacy of the ordinances of the church is the OPERATION OF THE SPIRIT. He makes the word and the sacraments, past and present, come alive, and only He can.

The Jews' faith in the same Lord Jesus Christ brought for them, as for Christians today, FULL REMISSION OF THEIR SINS AND ETERNAL SALVATION. This was no partial remission or "passing over" of sins, no mere promise of forgiveness when the promised Messiah came, no hope of a later salvation, but a FULL REMISSION. Therefore THIS ADMINISTRATION IS CALLED THE OLD TESTAMENT, because the efficacy of the blood of Jesus Christ was administered in, by, and through the blood of bulls and goats. The lambs were taking away the sin of the world of that time, because the Lamb of God was taking away the sin of the world at that time.

7.6 Under the gospel the same Covenant of Grace comes, but by fewer ordinances, more simply administered, to more people (ALL NATIONS), and MORE FULLY DEVELOPED, so that we have ONE AND THE SAME COVENANT UNDER DIFFERENT DISPENSATIONS. It is clear that the *Westminster Confession* holds to the traditional "modal" differences between the old and the new dispensations. The Covenant of Grace now has: FEWER ordinances, more simplicity of administration, "more fullness," more "evidence," more "spiritual efficacy," and more people to whom administered. Covenant theology does not deny significant differences between ancient Israel and the church.

Of these six conditional differences three (fewer ordinances, more simplicity of administration, and more people to whom administered) hardly require comment, but the other three do. "More fullness" well describes the Lord's Supper, which more fully pictures the sacrifice of Jesus Christ than a thousand dying lambs. Christ's death is the demonstrative "evidence" that it was indeed a divine Lamb of God who would take away the sins of the world. The Spirit of God works more mightily, deeply, extensively, and continually than He did in the bygone dispensation—that is, with more "spiritual efficacy" indeed.

The central affirmation of this chapter, for which the *Confession* and the entire seventeenth century are famous, is: THERE ARE NOT THEN TWO ESSENTIALLY DIFFERENT COVENANTS OF GRACE, BUT ONE AND THE SAME COVENANT UNDER DIFFERENT DISPENSATIONS. Difference of "mode" but identity of "substance" is the perpetual formula of covenant theology. Difference of mode has been challenged by Seventh Day Adventists, past as well as present, while sameness of substance has been rejected by dispensationalists, past and present. But for covenant theologians, past and present, the Covenant of Grace has differed in administration but was, is, and ever shall be the same in substance, that substance being nothing other than "the Lamb of God slain before the foundation of the world" (Rev 13.8).

Chapter 8

Concerning Christ the Mediator

This chapter tells us that the Son of God, being eternally chosen to be mediator, by the incarnation added the human to His divine nature. In His human nature He was obedient to death and, having made satisfaction for the sins of the elect, gloriously exalted. This satisfaction was effectually applied to and wrought in the elect even before it was purchased for them.

8.1 As mediator for the redemption of the people given to Him, the Son of God was appointed to many offices. This first paragraph lists them: PROPHET, PRIEST, KING, HEAD AND SAVIOR OF THE CHURCH, HEIR OF ALL THINGS, and JUDGE OF THE WORLD.

As prophet Christ enlightens the world, especially those for whom He died as priest and whom He brings to and keeps for Himself as king. He thereby becomes the head and savior of the SEED given to Him. Christ also became the heir of all things, including the world He judges. "All things are yours," Paul says to the church (1 Cor 3.21), because Christ inherits everything for the church's sake, including those who are not His own. The sole purpose of all these glorious offices is to receive the seed given Him from eternity. The Mediator's errand in this world was to redeem that seed; His atonement was specifically designed for that reason.

The redemption of the elect includes what Reformed theologians have always called the Golden Chain: foreloving, predestinating, calling, justifying, sanctifying, and glorifying.

8.2 Now to the Son's being. His person is one: divine. His natures are two: divine and human. The human nature is taken from the Virgin Mary without her sinfulness and with the result that these two natures, human and divine, although inseparable, are "without conversion" (or without ALTERING either nature into the other), "without composition" (or without being merely merged so that they are in fact DISUNITED, and so cannot constitute one true person), or "without confusion" (i.e. without mixing the two natures together into a third which is neither fully divine nor fully human). Thus Jesus is TRULY GOD AND TRULY MAN. The *Confession* shows itself here to be in agreement with the orthodox, Chalcedonian, catholic Christology of the Christian ages.

The position that the two natures are inseparable denies the Nestorian heresy of the early church, to which Socinianism, Liberalism, Christian Science, and other modern heresies approximate. If it seems strange to make such a comparison to modern liberal theology, it is because Liberalism separates deity far more thoroughly than ancient Nestorianism did from Jesus of Nazareth.

On the other hand the position that the two natures are "without conversion, composition, or confusion" (not ALTERED, DISUNITED OR MIXED TOGETHER) denies the ancient (and modern) heresies of Monophysitism and Monothelitism, which hold that the two natures or wills are made into one nature or will and are thereby confused. These heresies, which virtually deny the true humanity of Jesus, are still widespread in the Orient. Of course, they make it very difficult for their adherents to take the example of Jesus practically.

Note that the true human nature of the incarnate Son is derived from the true human SUBSTANCE of the Virgin Mary. It would have been unnecessary for the *Confession* to have explicitly stated that the incarnation was "without sin" were it not assuming that Mary herself was *not* "without sin." The heresy of the sinlessness of Mary is relatively recent, dating from the late Middle Ages. On the other hand the virgin birth, which is taught plainly in Scripture, has been affirmed by the church from the very earliest time in the forerunners of the Apostles' Creed.

The final statement in this paragraph, that Jesus is THE ONLY MEDIATOR BETWEEN GOD AND MAN, was taken bodily from the Scriptures (1 Tm 2.5).

8.3 Here we see that, although Christ was TRULY GOD, as man He was as dependent on God as any other man. As mediator, He was also blessed by God with God the Holy Spirit, Who fully indwelt Him.

It was God's pleasure that Christ be COMPLETELY EQUIPPED for his office. Even Christ could not take His office on Himself but like any other minister WAS CALLED TO IT. So, as mediator, Christ was absolutely dependent on God the Father. It may reasonably be asked if this is not the same as saying that Christ was dependent on Himself, since He is God. The answer is yes and no. Yes, insofar as He is divine and fully divine in essence. No, insofar as in the Covenant of Redemption Christ voluntarily subordinated Himself to the Father as executive. In that sense the Son as God no less than as man was dependent on the will of the Father.

8.4 Here the working out of Jesus' office as mediator is outlined. In this work He actively fulfilled the Law and passively suffered in soul and body, including death and interment. Thereafter exalted, Jesus rose from the dead, ascended into heaven, makes intercession, and will return as judge of the world.

Note first that all of the aspects of Jesus' humiliation and exaltation pertain to His humanity, since His deity is incapable either of humiliation or exaltation. Although the language of active and passive obedience is not used here (as it is later), both the ideas that Christ satisfied the Law by meeting its demands for fulfillment and that He vicariously suffered punishment for sinners, seem to be implied.

In His exalted state Christ is continually making intercession for those for whom He died. This is how He applies the atonement made for them, and this explains why believers, although forgiven, continue to ask for the forgiveness of their sins. Christ is busily and gladly bringing His sacrifice before the Father's throne on their behalf. And indeed this is what makes the prayers of the saints acceptable. Christ prays for their prayers. John Chrysostom once told of a father who was about to return from a long journey. His young son gathered a bouquet from the garden to give him. But before he gave his father the bouquet, mother removed all the weeds, trimmed the stems, and arranged the flowers properly. In the same way Christ makes the prayers of the righteous avail.

The Second Coming of Christ is part of His mediatorial ministry. It's not over, as they say, until it's over. The *Confession* is eschatologically oriented.

8.5 Here the result of Christ's mediation is described. The Lord's obedience and sacrifice add up to the satisfaction of the Father, which brings both the corresponding blessing of reconciliation (the removal of offenses) and inheritance (the bringing of divine approval). The general terms of these twin blessings (negative and positive), deliverance from death and bestowal of life, will be seen more clearly in the discussion of justification in Chapter 11.

This section notes again that atonement is limited; Christ's mediatorial benefits are only for those WHOM THE FATHER HAS GIVEN TO HIM. We also see that the EVERLASTING INHERITANCE was not earned by Christians but that their rewards are a result of pure grace. Here too is an interesting allusion to the eternal continuance of the KINGDOM OF HEAVEN and the fulfillment of the prayer, "Thy kingdom come." The kingdom exists now and is "within you" (Lk 17.21), and yet it is also the sphere of an EVERLASTING INHERITANCE.

8.6 Here is a fuller and more explicit statment about the efficacy of the atonement in past dispensations, tracing it all the way back to the fall of man. First of all, Christ was not literally SLAIN FROM THE BEGINNING OF THE WORLD but the POWER, EFFECTIVENESS, AND BENEFITS of His death were from the foundation of the world. Young people especially often ask about the salvation of Old Testament believers (and usually they get the wrong answer). The answer is as clear here as in the proof text cited, Romans 3.25. They are saved just as believers after the death of Christ are saved and have the same salvation – by the sacrifice of Christ! No *limbus patrum* (place where Old Testament saints are supposed to have waited until Christ died) is found in the *Westminster Confession* or in the Bible.

The protoevangelium (Gen 3.15) is recognized as just that: the earliest preaching of the gospel of Jesus Christ. Since Christ is the same yesterday, today, and forever, the gospel does not change either, nor the salvation by it. How dispensationalism could ever consider itself compatible with the *Westminster Confession* is mystifying.

8.7 The humiliation and exaltation Christ underwent in His mediatorial ministry also involved His deity. This paragraph articulates the famous doctrine of the "community of attributes" (*koinonia idiomatum*). Here again the *Confession* reveals its oneness with traditional orthodoxy on fundamental doctrines. CHRIST ACTS ACCORDING TO BOTH HIS NATURES. It does not say here, however, what the different acts were coming from EACH NATURE DOING WHAT IS PROPER TO EACH. It is apparent, though, that by acts in the human nature we must think of Christ eating, sleeping, suffering, dying, etc. Allusions to the divine nature would be: "He who has seen me has seen the Father" (Jn 10:30); "Before Abraham was I am" (Jn 8.58); etc.

The statement that SCRIPTURE SOMETIMES ATTRIBUTES WHAT IS PROPER TO ONE NATURE TO THE PERSON INDICATED BY THE OTHER NATURE is illustrated by Acts 20.28: "the church of God which He purchased with His own blood." Here God is said to have blood. We know, of course, that Scripture teaches plainly that God is a Spirit, and spirits do not have blood. The reference is clear, however. It is to the death of Jesus Christ in His human nature. Christ was a genuine human being, and He had genuine red blood coursing through His human body. That blood was shed on Calvary. But although that blood was of His human nature, because that nature was indissolubly united with His divine person, the text here in Acts refers to the blood of God — a classic illustration of the community of attributes.

8.8 Here the point is made that Christ takes all the appropriate steps for bringing this great mediatorial work to the SEED God gave Him BY HIS ALMIGHTY POWER AND WISDOM. He: MAKES INTERCESSION, REVEALS, PERSUADES, GOVERNS, and OVERCOMES . . . ENEMIES.

Since all Christ's mediatorial work as prophet and priest would have been in vain had He not applied it, His office of king is crucial. We also see clearly here that Christ not only died for His people but lives in them and thereby brings them to live with Him forever. The conclusion of this paragraph is the proper introduction to what follows in the next chapters. We are told generally here and in detail subsequently about the the way the great mediatorial work of Christ is *applied* to those for whom He performed it.

Chapter 9

Concerning Free Will

The five rather short paragraphs here teach us that man has a NATURAL or non-forced ability, which before the fall included a power to will the good but which after the fall was lost, so that now man cannot even prepare himself to choose the good of the gospel. That power cannot be restored except by enabling GRACE, and even then it is not perfected until it is perfected in heaven.

9.1 Here we see that in the beginning God gave man an unforced, unnecessitated will either to good or evil. Although it does not make the point explicitly, apparently the *Confession* means that free will, in the sense of not forced will, was an inalienable NATURAL endowment of man as man. Since this "liberty" or freedom of will is inalienable or natural, it is an unlosable part of the definition of man and would characterize man in heaven, earth, or hell. In this respect neither Reformed theology nor the *Westminster Confession* are determinist in the sense of behaviorist, coercive, or fatalistic.

9.2 In innocency before the fall man had the moral ability TO WILL AND TO DO WHAT IS GOOD AND PLEASING TO GOD, but he also had the possibility of losing that ability.

Note first that the *Confession* uses the term STATE OF INNOCENCE quite differently from much contemporary usage. Today the expression often refers to man as created, but created in a state of indifference, inclining *neither* to good nor to evil. As we have seen, according to the *Confession*, man was created righteous. His innocence was of any wrongdoing, not of any right-inclining. He was by nature inclined to righteousness. The problem then, alluded to earlier, is how, being inclined to the good, man chose evil. But the problem is even greater for those moderns who think that in innocence man was inclined to neither, since they have to explain how it was that man came to choose either good or evil.

In the reasoning of the *Confession*, although man was righteous and inclined to the good, not being unchangeable as is the good God, he was capable of changing from his good will. This states the fact but does not explain why man, since he was inclined only to the good, even though he was capable of changing, would ever have chosen to change. However, the *Confession* is certainly correct in its teaching, although not explaining it, because that is what the Bible itself teaches. There can be no higher proof of anything than that it is taught by God's word, whether that word condescends to explain it to us mortals or not.

9.3 This paragraph outlines a complete post mortem of the human victim of the fall. Man has fallen INTO A STATE OF SIN, is incapable of ANY SPIRITUAL GOOD, is in fact OPPOSED to it, and is therefore DEAD and UNABLE to resurrect HIMSELF to spiritual life.

First here is what is commonly called the doctrine of moral inability. Fallen man is still able — able to will evil, in fact very able to do so all the time and exclusively — but totally unable at any time to will any good whatever. He not only does not do good, but he is also incapable of good, in the sense of being indisposed toward any good. This doctrine is applied as well and especially to the gospel. The sinner is disinclined to any good including — especially including — the gospel offer. But not only is the sinner disinclined he is also COMPLETELY OPPOSED to the gospel. He not only does not come to Christ but drives Christ away from him. As one Reformed theologian put it: man would kill God if he could, but since he cannot, he kills Christians instead, when he can.

Even further, not only can the sinner not CONVERT HIM- SELF, he cannot even PREPARE HIMSELF FOR CONVER- SION. This statement is meant to deny the Roman Catholic doctrine of works of congruity not the Puritan doctrine of preparation. The former teaches that the unconverted can do things that ingratiate the deity, inclining Him to bestow grace congruous with their good works. The Puritan doctrine, on the other hand, teaches that although everything sinners do before conversion is sinful (even going to church), however, going to church may precede an utterly unmerited, gracious, *incon*gruous act of saving grace.

9.4 This section describes what happens in divine conversion. Delivered from his bondage to sin and being brought into a state of grace, the sinner now has his lost ability to will the good restored, without, at the same time, losing his acquired ability to will the evil.

The basic point here is that it is only God who changes sinners. The sinner cannot convert himself or even take steps in that direction. The sinner's extremity is God's opportunity, which He graciously chooses to take. Note also that it is not only at the time of conversion that God enables a sinner to choose the good, but it is GOD'S GRACE ALONE that ever enables him TO WILL AND TO DO WHAT IS SPIRITUALLY GOOD for his entire converted life. Grace operates in sanctification no less than in justification.

But now the battle of Romans 7 begins. Before conversion the sinner was consistently and uniformly sinful. But now he wills both good and evil—because of his OLD SINFUL NATURE which, although dying, is far from dead.

9.5 This battle rages throughout life. Moral freedom to choose the GOOD ALONE comes only at death.

On first reading, it looks like the Westminster divines made a mistake in this paragraph, when they assert that in glory the "will of man is made . . . immutably free to good alone." They seem to have forgotten their own doctrine that God alone is immutable, i.e. UNCHANGEABLE (2.1). Man's will never becomes *in itself* immutable. What the *Confession* probably means is that the will of man is *kept by God* perfectly and immutably free to good alone in the state of glory only. This

Biblical promise is what the Westminster theologians and all Christians are counting on, and this is the great difference between Adam in the garden and Adam in heaven. In heaven man is forever and forever *non posse peccare*! We must remember, however, that man always (in hell as well as heaven) retains his *natural* ability to choose. Fallen man in hell has lost his *moral* ability ever to choose good. In heaven, perfected believers have lost their *moral* ability to choose evil.

Chapter 10

Concerning Effectual Calling

Salvific human action begins in this chapter. Up to this point the *Confession* has been discussing the nature and purposes of God and man. With EFFECTUAL CALLING the predestinated, while still passive, are graciously changed and brought savingly to embrace Christ in the gospel (or without hearing it in the cases of elect, dying infants and others not outwardly called). At the same time some of the non-elect hear the message and receive some influences of the Spirit but NEVER TRULY COME and therefore cannot be saved, as is true of those who only live by the light of nature.

10.1 By means of the word and the Spirit those predestinated are called into a state of grace. Their minds are enlightened, their hearts are changed, and their wills are renewed. They are thus drawn willingly. Those who think that predestination is unnecessary in true preaching are here reminded that it is precisely the predestinated who are effectually called by the word (and the Spirit). Preaching is a part of predestination.

Those who think that irresistible grace means being dragged against one's will are also reminded here that what is involved is being drawn *willingly* as a result of an enlightened mind, changed heart, and renewed will. There is really no such thing as a forced will any more than a squared circle. If it is a will, it is not forced; if it is forced, it is not a will. Were a man to tell one of us to stop writing this or have a bullet put through the brain, he would not be forcing one of our wills, because we might choose to go on writing, if that were more important than living. In the same way, if your heart is changed by the Spirit of God, nothing outside you drags you to Christ. It is your new will that lovingly embraces Him.

10.2 This section points out that there is nothing God foresees in man that brings about divine conversion. Man is passive when brought to life by the Holy Spirit, who thereby enables him to ANSWER and embrace the grace offered. This doctrine is pure, Reformed, Augustinian, monergistic, regeneration. It is one work (God's alone) — not two (man cooperating) — bringing the dead sinner to life. It is nothing "foreseen in man" because there is nothing but deadness to be foreseen in man, apart from divine regeneration.

The Calvinistic "Methodist" George Whitefield showed himself to be an eloquent advocate of effectual calling, when, speaking on Ephesians 2.1 following, he likened the sinner to dead Lazarus called from the grave.

> Come, ye dead, Christless, unconverted sinners, come and see the place where they laid the body of the deceased Lazarus; behold him laid out, bound hand and foot with graveclothes, locked up and stinking in a dark cave, with a great stone placed on the top of it. View him again and again; go nearer to him; be not afraid; smell him. Ah! how he stinketh. Stop there now, pause a while; and whilst thou art gazing upon the corpse of Lazarus, give me leave to tell thee with great plainness, but greater love, that this dead, bound, entombed, stinking carcase, is but a faint representation of thy poor soul in its natural state: for . . . thy spirit which thou bearest about with thee, sepulchred in flesh and blood, is as literally dead to God, and as truly dead in trespasses and sins, as the body of Lazarus was in the cave. Was he bound hand and foot with graveclothes? So art thou bound hand and foot with thy corruptions: and as a stone was laid on the sepulchre, so is there a stone of unbelief upon thy stupid heart. Perhaps thou has lain in this state, not only four days, but many years, stinking in God's nostrils. And, what is still more effecting, thou art as unable to raise thyself out of this loathsome, dead state, to a life of righteousness and true holiness, as ever Lazarus was to raise himself from the cave in which he lay so long. Thou mayest try the

power of thy own boasted free will, and the force and energy of moral persuasion and rational arguments (which, without all doubt, have their proper place in religion); but all thy efforts, exerted with never so much vigor, will prove quite fruitless and abortive, till that same Jesus, who said "take away the stone" and cried "Lazarus, come forth," also quicken you.

This is grace, graciously offered, and grace graciously applied. Or as the *Confession* originally puts it, "grace offered and conveyed."

10.3 Elect dying infants and some adults INCAPABLE OF BEING OUTWARDLY CALLED may be regenerated by the sovereignly working Spirit of God. Faith, of course, usually comes by hearing (Rom 10.17), but the Spirit may sovereignly work apart from the usual means where these means are not available. The *Confession* does not know who or how many are the fortunate recipients of this unusual working of the Holy Spirit but gives us this paragraph to extol the unlimited activity of the One who like the wind moves as He wills (Jn 3.8). Note that contrary to modern extensions of the saving activity of the Holy Spirit to *all* those dying in infancy the *Confession* asserts that only ELECT INFANTS, DYING IN INFANCY are thus regenerated. There is a current tendency to drop unconsciously the word "elect" from the confessional statement. Westminster does *not* deny that *all* dying in infancy *may* be elect, although that may be implied.

There has also been modern debate about so-called anonymous Christians, i.e. putative Christians belonging to other religions or no religion, who, it is said, are Christians without really knowing what Christianity is. The statement here in the *Confession* does allow for this phenomenon, but not in the way it is commonly, almost promiscuously, used today to regard any serious moral person belonging to any religion or no religion at all as a born-again Christian.

10.4 The non-elect, who, being called and even those having common operations of the Spirit, do not TRULY COME and CANNOT BE SAVED. Certainly those who are not even called, although they may frame their lives "according to the light of nature" (ACCORDING TO THEIR OWN UNDERSTANDING) cannot be saved. To say that they can is indeed a HORRIBLE SUGGESTION. This is not to deny Acts 17.27.

There are a couple of minor faults in the way this section is expressed. The non-regenerate are not really CALLED, as has been explained above, and sinners never really "frame their lives according to the light of nature" anyway. Romans 1.20 and following emphatically maintain that the unregenerate *suppress* the light of nature.

The recognition the *Confession* makes here of common operations of the Spirit that are *non-saving* is much needed in our church today, a church not noted, unfortunately, for careful distinctions. It is all too quickly and erroneously assumed now that *any* activity of the Holy Spirit is evidence of regeneration. Not so!

In this context it is also very salutary to be reminded that many who profess faith NEVER TRULY COME TO CHRIST. Walter Martin, the late specialist in cults, has said that there are ten different definitions of Christ circulating among us. G. K. Chesterton contends that most Christians today do not know what Christianity is and that, if they ever find out, they will discover that they do not like it. It has also been noted by some that most Christians today do not believe in the virgin birth, the deity of Christ, or the Trinity. Such people are not, of course, really Christians, and it is still lamentably true that many professed Christians NEVER TRULY COME TO CHRIST AND THEREFORE CANNOT BE SAVED.

Our own age and many modern professing Christians will also be offended by the last point in this section which denies that anyone can be saved by trying to follow THE TENETS OF SOME OTHER RELIGION. Our age likes to think (erroneously) that any sincere attempt to follow any religion or moral code is enough to save. But Jesus is the only way (Jn 14.6, Acts 4.12, and frequently). Human sincerity per se reaps no salvation. (Himmler was very sincere. He was sincerely devoted to Hitler and sincerely determined to exterminate the Jews.)

Chapter 11

Concerning Justification

Everyone knows that justification by faith alone is, as Martin Luther said to the Parliament of Worms in 1521, "the doctrine by which the church stands or falls." This chapter would convince Luther that the church of the *Westminster Confession* is still standing! It teaches that those who are effectually called to faith are freely justified by Christ—only, however, by the instrumentality of their working faith. Although the decree and the death of Christ are in the past, the justification of those who are effectually called does not occur until their faith, in union with Christ, keeps them as penitent believers.

11.1 Justification is not by any righteousness infused into the believer but by Christ's righteousness imputed to the believer and received by the divine gift of faith, bestowed in effectual calling. This doctrine is what primarily distinguishes the Reformation church from the Roman Catholic church. Rome kept the name justification but changed the Biblical meaning from the justification by the *righteousness of Christ imputed* through faith to the *righteousness of the believer wrought* through faith—a momentous difference, which can be simply illustrated as follows.

Roman Catholicism: Faith + Works → Justification
Protestantism: Faith → Justification + Works

There is still another basic difference between the Protestant and Roman positions. According to the Reformers faith is a GIFT OF GOD; according to Roman Catholicism it is the work of man, in two distinct ways. First, it is the person's unregenerate decision which brings him or her to baptism, and that in turn, along with the Spirit, produces regeneration. And so, in the Roman view, it is the sinner who brings about his own salvation. Secondly, even after this regeneration, faith itself occurs by the non-resisting cooperation of the believer.

11.2 Although the person is justified by faith alone, this faith is never alone but is ALWAYS ACCOMPANIED BY ALL THE OTHER SAVING GRACES. Here is the other side of the justification coin. It focuses not on faith alone but on *faith associated*. Both sides of the truth of justification are as essential to the doctrine of justification as justification is essential to salvation. Section 1 exposes the fatal Roman Catholic error. This section exposes an equally fatal deviation among Protestants — so-called Protestants, that is. The proper name is Antinomianism.

If we put Antinomian teaching in the same kind of graphic display, it comes out like this:

Faith → Justification − Works

Antinomianism makes too little of works, just as Roman Catholicism makes too much of them. Rome makes works the *basis* of justification; antinomianism dispenses with them as *necessary accompaniments* to justification. Luther wrote two treatises against antinomianism. Were he living today, he might have written twenty-two.

11.3 Justification glorifies God's PERFECT JUSTICE and His RICH GRACE, because it is based on Christ's satisfaction, which is freely given and NOT FOR ANYTHING IN those who receive it. Section 1 is a statement of the truth of justification against Romanism and section 2 a statement of the truth of justification against Antinomianism. Section 3 is a statement of the truth of justification against Socinianism or its current form, Liberalism (Modernism).

Liberalism argues that free justification based on satisfaction is a contradiction in terms; it is like a paid-for gift. The answer to this objection is, of course, clearly stated here in section 3. The *gift* is free to the recipient, but it is at the same time paid-for-in-full by the divine *Giver*. Liberalism teaches another gospel, which can be represented this way:

Works → Justification − Faith

Liberalism *does* believe in faith in just about everything — except the SATISFACTION of Jesus Christ. It is revolted by what it characterizes (or rather caricatures) as a bloody religion of an alienated and angry God who must by propitiated by the sacrifice of an innocent victim in the place of guilty sinners. While Liberalism says "ugh" to its own caricature of the gospel, true Evangelicalism glories in the cross of Christ where justice and mercy kiss each other.

11.4 Although decreed in eternity and accomplished centuries ago on a cross outside a city wall, justification does not come to the elect UNTIL THE HOLY SPIRIT IN DUE TIME DOES ACTUALLY APPLY CHRIST TO THEM. The *Confession* is very conscious of the fact that the golden chain of salvation was forged in eternity. Nevertheless, it insists here that it touches the elect only at the appointed time in history, the time that saving faith is born. Some great Reformed theologians (e.g. A. A. Hodge and Abraham Kuyper) have disagreed and staunchly defended what is denied here. We honor their obvious desire to glorify God by their contention. However, in this case the *Confession* seems rightly to insist on the Bible's teaching that justification is by *faith*, which is clearly *not* eternal.

It should be noted here that the Reformed faith, so systematically and accurately stated by the *Westminster Confession* (as well as many other creeds), has a great unity among its theologians. The differences are few and, while not unimportant, are highly technical and little known by the rank and file of believers. Eternal justification is one of these differences.

11.5 Here is still another facet of the many-splendored doctrine of justification. Although justification is a *fait accompli,* forgiveness CONTINUES as FATHERLY DISPLEASURE with believers brings them to ASK FOR FORGIVENESS AND RENEW THEIR FAITH IN REPENTANCE. The justified, being forgiven, must continue to ask for (draw on) their forgiven-ness. This ray of justification truth also has its shadow of misrepresentation in the distortion of "once forgiven, always forgiven." Therefore, some erroneously say that we need not and cannot pray "forgive us our debts," not, that is, in this dispensation of grace. Furthermore, they say that it is legal ground to ask forgiveness as "we forgive others," and so they do not pray the Lord's prayer.

Thus Antinomianism raises its heretical head again. It maintains that we may be forgiven without forgiving and without even asking to be forgiven for not forgiving. By contrast the correct formula articulated here in the *Confession* is: once forgiven, one continues to ask the same forgiveness for new sins and shortcomings even as he continues forgiving new sins and shortcomings in those around and against him.

11.6 This brief statement that THE JUSTIFICATION OF BELIEVERS UNDER THE OLD TESTAMENT WAS IN ALL THESE RESPECTS IDENTICAL WITH THE JUSTIFICATION OF BELIEVERS UNDER THE NEW TESTAMENT has been fully explained and elaborated earlier.

Chapter 12

Concerning Adoption

With only one section, this chapter is the briefest in the *Westminster Confession*. However, it includes a shopping list of benefits wrapped up in that one gracious package, adoption. This is the list:

(a) the liberties and privileges of being God's children,

(b) the name of God being put on them,

(c) the Spirit of adoption,

(d) bold access to the throne of grace,

(e) the right to call God, "Abba," Father,

(f) being pitied, protected, provided for, and disciplined by the Father,

(g) never cast off,

(h) sealed to the day of redemption, and

(i) inheriting the promises of everlasting salvation.

Jonathan Edwards has eloquently put the ribbon of "union with Christ" around this divine package in an early *Miscellany*.

By virtue of the believer's union with Christ, he doth really possess all things . . . .. I mean that God, three in one, all that he is, and all that he has, and all that he does, all that he has made or done, the whole universe, bodies and spirits, light, heaven, angels, men and devils, sun, moon, stars, land, sea, fish and fowls, all the silver and gold, kings and potentates, as well as mere men, are as much the Christian's as the money in his pocket, the clothes he wears, or the house he dwells in, as the victuals he eats; yea, more properly his, more advantageoulsly, more his than if he commands all those things mentioned to be just in all respects as he pleased, at any time, by virtue of the union with Christ, because Christ who certainly doth thus possess all things is entirely his, so that he possesses it all . . . . only he has not the trouble of managing of it but

Christ to whom it is no trouble, manages it for him, a thousand times as much to his advantage as he could himself, if he had the managing of all . . .. And who would desire to possess all things more than to have all things managed just according to his will . . .?

Chapter 13

Concerning Sanctification

Sanctification has been called the "Christianizing of the Christian." Here it is described in three stages: (1) the implantation of the NEW HEART by Christ's power and its MORE AND MORE destroying the POWER OF SIN; (2) the resultant war between the two principles; and (3) the outcome of that war, which is certain victory for the new creation.

13.1 This first section gives an overview of sanctification. It teaches that sanctification means acquiring a NEW HEART or SPIRIT and an additional sanctification from the efficacy of Christ's work (as well as His word and Spirit indwelling) so that the old "dominion" of sin is destroyed and its remaining lusts gradually overcome as greater and greater holiness within leads to holy outward practice. Six specific aspects of sanctification are mentioned here:
  (a) a NEW HEART or SPIRIT being given,
  (b) real, personal sanctification — meaning realized
       holiness by virtue of Christ's work and presence,
  (c) "dominion" of sin broken,
  (d) remaining DESIRES more and more WEAKENED,
  (e) the sanctified person being more and more sanctified
       (in ALL THE GRACES), and
  (f) manifestation of sanctification in indispensable
       practice.

13.2 Here treatment of the details of sanctification begins with emphasis on the fact that sanctification occurs in THE WHOLE PERSON. Remaining sin is, of course, also in the whole person, and consequently we have the life-long (CONTINUAL) war in our members. Corruption then as well as holiness is in the total person, who is not free of either, in the mind or the body. Each of us must cultivate piety and resist pollution in the spirit no less than sensually. The Westminster divines then reject the classical view that virtue is in the mind and vice in the body, so that the moral struggle is between the physical and the spiritual.

R. L. Stevenson's presentation of Dr. Jekyl and Mr. Hyde does not reflect a Christian view of morality. In Stevenson's story the struggle is betwen the pride of life and the bodily appetites — i.e. between one lust and another lust. The Christian struggle in sanctification is between the Holy Spirit and the evil spririt, whether of body or mind.

There is a question here about what *spirit* is struggling. The original *Westminster Confession* has "the flesh lusting against the spirit." Our modern version has: THE OLD NATURE TRIES TO GET ITS WAY IN OPPOSITION TO THE SPIRIT [the Spirit]. In Galatians 5:17, from which this language originally comes, it cannot be determined by the word itself whether *pneuma* is to be translated "spirit" or "Spirit." From the context of this passage it is probably the latter. If so, then the struggle is between the Holy Spirit and the remaining corruption in each regenerate person, simply identified as "flesh" (*sarx*). This would not, of course, exclude the sanctified human spirit being moved by the divine Spirit, and "struggles" or FIGHTS must be understood anthropomorphically and not literally. The Spirit of God, who Himself created all things out of nothing, does not need to struggle literally with that which He has made out of nothing. However, He permits the struggle to take place as He graciously and gradually subjugates the remaining rebellion in believers' members.

Finally, any notion of perfectionism is also dispelled in this section. The new heart breaks the "dominion" but does not eradicate the presence of sin. As long as sin remains, perfection is impossible.

13.3 In spite of temporary setbacks, victory is certain, because the Holy Spirit continues to enable believers to grow. Although none of us has ever escaped lost BATTLES IN THIS

WARFARE, THE REGENERATE NATURE is destined TO OVERCOME in every Christian, past, present, and future.

Note that PERFECT HOLINESS proceeds IN THE FEAR OF GOD. As Paul tells us, it is to be worked out with "fear and trembling" (Phil 2.12). Why the fear, since the victory is certain? Chapter 17 on perseverance answers this more fully, but here it can be pointed out that the old nature is so omnipresent, powerful, victorious in battles (if not the war) that the believer must watch and pray every step of his sanctified way through a field sewn with explosives. He knows he will arrive safely, but there is danger every step of the way.

Chapter 14

Concerning Saving Faith

This chapter tells us how faith is produced, what it accomplishes, what its activities are, and how its varying degrees are related to the assurance of salvation.

14.1 The Spirit of God works saving faith in the elect, ordinarily by the word (strengthening it by the same word), by the sacraments, and by prayer. Here is the *divine initiative*, a distinctive feature of Reformed theology. Arminian evangelism asserts to the contrary that man produces the faith—not without the aid of the Holy Spirit—which is then followed by regeneration and is subsequently strengthened by the word, sacraments, and prayer. But the Bible indicates that man must *first* be born again, before he can enter the kingdom of God (Jn 3.3,5). The divine initiative, however, is not independent of the word. "Faith comes" (when the Spirit comes) . . . "by the word" (Rom 10.17), which usually comes (as we shall see later) in the form of preaching when the Spirit energizes it.

The evangelist, then, sews the seed, but it is God, the Spirit, who gives the increase. Even Lutherans, who construe Hebrews 4.12 as teaching that the word itself produces faith (if not resisted), seem to forget that only the Spirit can make the word sharper than a two-edged sword. It is the Spirit who wields His sword, the word (Eph 6.17).

According to the *Confession*, after faith is born in the souls of the elect, it is increased by the sacraments and prayer. The meaning here is apparently that the Holy Spirit then uses these as well as the word in working and continuing faith.

14.2 The general effect of the Spirit's work is to produce faith in WHATEVER IS REVEALED IN THE WORD, because it is God's word, while faith's CHIEF ACTIONS are trusting in Christ for the benefits of the Covenant of Grace.

The Roman Catholic doctrine of *implicit faith* teaches that Catholics accept all that their church officially teaches implicitly, even before they learn what it is. This is a travesty of the true doctrine here presented in the *Westminster Confession* — regenerate Christians have faith in the word of God, not in the word of men. Implicit faith in the Scripture is actually what the Spirit works in the hearts of the elect. Before they understand or even read what the Bible says, they know it is true because of its divine authority. When they read it, they *know* it is the word of God and accept it as such.

The various responses of the elect — submitting, trembling, embracing — according to the teaching of Scripture show the experiential character of this knowledge. Such responses are thus evidence of the indwelling, saving presence of the Spirit of God. However, the CHIEF acts are the resting on Christ for the various benefits of the Covenant of Grace. We presume the *Confession* designates these acts CHIEF, because they are of ultimate importance for our salvation. In a sense, all Christian responses to the word worked by the Holy Spirit are directly or indirectly, immediately or reflexively, a resting on Christ alone for salvation.

Note that the *Confession* does not make explicit here the *testimonium spiritus sancti*, the internal testimony of the Holy Spirit, the doctrine for which the Reformed tradition and especially John Calvin are famous. This doctrine had already been articulated in the first chapter.

14.3 Although worked by the Spirit, faith is still weak and assailed from time to time. However, it grows even to full assurance in many believers, because it comes from Christ, its Creator and ultimate Perfecter.

After rejoicing in the work of the Holy Spirit in the hearts of the elect, the *Confession*, brings us back to earth in pointing out one effect of the sin which remains in the hearts even of the regenerate. Christ is in our hearts but so is the world, the flesh, and devil. Since sanctification involves warfare, we should not be surprised that its citadel, faith, is under constant attack. Since it is vulnerable in the imperfect believer, it is not only under attack but WEAKENED. But, in spite of this weakness and the hardness of its opponents, such is the strength of faith's *author and finisher* that MANY BELIEVERS become COMPLETELY ASSURED by it. Not all who have faith have assurance, but not a few do. So, we learn that there may be true faith without assurance but also assurance without perfection.

Chapter 15

Concerning Repentance Leading to Life

Repentance, which must be preached, turns a sinner from his sin not only because of its DANGER but also its "odiousness" to that new walk without which one is not pardoned. Since no sin is too small to damn the impenitent or too great to damn the penitent, men must repent of particular sins, confessing privately to God and men (publicly where necessary) in order to be reconciled.

15.1 It seems strange that the *Westminster Confession* should make a specific point of repentance being preached, when the whole counsel of God must be preached. Perhaps there was a tendency in the seventeenth century, as now, to eliminate the negative (repentance) and accentuate the positive (faith). Whatever the reason, it is as important to preach repentance from sin as to preach faith in the Savior. These are certainly inseparable, because it is impossible to have faith in Christ without turning from sin to Him or, on the other hand, to turn from sin without turning to Him.

15.2 Here the true nature of repentance is described. It is a turning from sin, in which the sin is accurately seen as FILTHY and against the very character of God; it grows out of an apprehension of mercy in Christ and includes a positive behaving according to God's commandments.

It probably cannot be emphasized enough that loathing the sinfulness of sin is essential to true repentance. The disadvantages of sin are much easier to recognize. But repenting of the consequences is not repenting of the sin itself. It is a common human experience to regret wrongdoing when faced with exposure and punishment. Our wrongdoing in those cases has proved embarrassing. But what we really regret is being caught, not being sinful. We are not really sorry for our sinful wrongdoing per se. Both Esau and Judas seem to have regretted the disadvantages of their sins without truly repenting. In one the result was worldliness and in the other suicide. Neither turned from their sins and started behaving differently, in a godly way.

While repentance of the consequences of sin do not lead to anything virtuous, true repentance from sin leads to our walking WITH HIM ACCORDING TO ALL HIS COMMANDMENTS. The results of repentance lead not to vice but virtue. If one begins living according to the divine commandments, there is repentance. On the other hand, if there is no change of behavior, there is no change of heart and no repentance.

Note that there is a hating and a turning. Both go together, and one without the other is futile and spurious. One may dislike sin and keep on doing it (and so not truly hate it). One may also turn from sin and not really hate it. Here again is turning from the consequences of sin rather than from sin itself. Repentance then, like every other divine grace, has its satanic counterfeit.

15.3 The meaning of this section is simply that repentance is non-meritoriously necessary. The true evangelical formula once again appears. Only now instead of:

Faith → Justification + Works

we have:

Repentance → Justification + Works.

If faith without works is dead, so is repentance without works. Yet, just as faith itself does not save, neither does repentance itself, but Christ only.

Here again we must have a correct understanding of legalism, one of a dozen or so terms continually used ambiguously — with incalculably and sometimes eternally harmful effects. Legalism has two meanings which must always be distinguished:

(1) Works as the meritorious basis of salvation, and
(2) Works as the non-meritorious accompaniment of
    salvation.

The first and really proper use of the term is the basis of a gospel entirely different from the true gospel of salvation in Christ. The second sense here involves a frequent but basically inaccurate usage; it is a benign "legalism," which is an essential mark of salvation. Consequently, when an action is described as "legalistic," there is usually the ambiguity of whether reference is being made to "another way of salvation" or to "a necessary accompaniment of the only true way of salvation." Frequently the reference will be to both in the common charge that another gospel is being taught by someone who claims that works are an obligation! Confusion often reigns, where clarity ought to.

Take the question of keeping the Sabbath. If someone tells a neighbor that he needs to keep the Sabbath, he may be referring to the legalism of 1 or 2. According to 1 he would mean that people are to be saved by the merit of Sabbath-keeping — a patently false and different gospel. According to 2 the meaning is that it is a duty to keep the Sabbath as evidence of one's true faith and repentance. The latter is debateable, of course, but later the *Westminster Confession* will argue that Sabbath-keeping is a duty. If we are so persuaded, then it is necessary for us to keep the Sabbath if we would be saved by the grace of God but not by any supposed merit in Sabbath-keeping.

15.4 The statement here could probably not be made more clearly or succinctly. Note that outside of Christ every sin, no matter how small, brings eternal damnation. But in Christ, every sin, no matter how great, never damns, provided it is not made a practice.

It might appear that the *Confession* has fallen here into the very Antinomianism it denounces. But it is not saying that *because* THERE IS NO SIN SO GREAT THAT IT CAN BRING DAMNATION UPON THOSE WHO TRULY REPENT a Christian may therefore sin as much and as greatly as he pleases. The

Confession has already made clear that anyone who sins as he pleases is not a Christian. What then is the meaning? It means that if a Christian is overtaken by a sin (not taken over), he will repent truly and repentantly amend his ways. David committed adultery; David was not an adulterer.

This classic, concise statement is also a rejection of the Roman Catholic distinction between venial and mortal sins. According to the *Confession* that is not a valid distinction. Every sin of an impenitent person is mortal, however small or "venial," and every sin of a penitent Christian, however great and "mortal," is venial or non-mortal.

15.5 It is not enough to be against sin generally. We must be specific, i.e. we must not be sorry in general but in particular. For example, while confessing our sins of omission, we should include explicit enumeration of: not writing that letter home, not remembering mother's birthday, not apologizing to that person we slighted, etc. The only limitation would be time. Just as the man, who fell from a window and was asked if it was true that while thinking death is inevitable all one's sins come rushing through the mind, answered that he had only fallen thirty feet not thirty miles, so our limitations, too, are only time.

When counseling about the genuineness of conversion and repentance in particular, ministers should probe deeply about the extent as well as the nature of repentance.

15.6 The rule here is that private confession to God is *always* necessary; public confession to the offended and/or to the church *may* be necessary. Note that the confession that *may* be considered necessary is necessary because whatever is not of faith is sin (Rom 14.23). That is, if we doubt whether we should or should not confess the fault, we have an obligation to confess it. But not every fault is to be confessed. Otherwise you would have time for nothing else. The faults, however, that are serious enough to make you wonder—about those you need not wonder, but confess.

Now if the repentance is because of the "filthiness" of the sin itself, you will have to acknowledge it to any person dirtied by it. Note finally that confession which should be private should not be made public. Christ says in Matthew 18.15ff that if one is offended he should ask satisfaction of the offender privately. Should the latter confess his fault, he is to be forgiven and the matter to end privately. Only when a serious fault is not acknowledged and corrected is it to be discussed with another indiviual present and so on to the church, if necessary. When James instructs us to confess our faults to one another (5.16), that means to *one* another and not to everybody. There has sometimes been great harm done to Christian causes by promiscuous confession — often of promiscuity.

Chapter 16

Concerning Good Works

This chapter, on good works, is one of the best works of the Westminster Assembly. Every aspect of the topic is definitively treated in seven paragraphs:

  (1) only what is commanded by God (in His word) is a good work;
  (2) the doing of such works is the fruit of the Spirit and fruitful every way;
  (3) the doing of them is wholly from the Spirit, but Christians are responsible for "stirring up" that grace;
  (4) far from supererogating what is required of believers, such works FALL SHORT of much of our duty;
  (5) far from deserving a reward, men's best works merit the severe judgment of God;
  (6) nevertheless, because believers are in Christ, these imperfect "good works" will actually receive a reward; and
  (7) unregenerate men can only do bad good works — bad, because of the evil hearts from which they spring, and good, only in the "matter of them."

16.1 It is clear that the *Confession* limits good works to God's works — God-commanded and God-worked. One wonders why duty which is revealed by the "light of nature" (God's nature) is excluded. Perhaps, it is because, as we shall see, only regenerate persons ever do good good works, however imperfect, and regeneration and sanctification only occur in connection with the word of God (and not the creation of God). No doubt this exclusiveness is designed to ward off the arrogance of men, especially clergymen, who fancy that they can command good works. All human authority is purely ministerial or declarative. That is, men in positions of authority are obligated to relay the commnandments of God. So their orders have authority not because they come *through* men but because they come *from* God. When, therefore, we obey men, it must be "as to the Lord" (Col 3.23). Otherwise it is not a good work, even though it should ultimately be commanded by God Himself. That is, since good works are God-works, we must *do* them, because they are God-commanded.

16.2 Having defined good works, the *Confession* says that the doing of them is the good work of the Holy Spirit moving believers and that in doing good works believers:
  (a) manifest thankfulness,
  (b) strengthen assurance,
  (c) edify fellow believers,
  (d) adorn their profession (i.e. of Christian faith),
  (e) silence criticisms,
  (f) glorify God (showing that their goodness is His work), and
  (g) bring eternal life.
Since good works come from a good root (the Spirit of God), they are consequently fruitful, full of good fruit. So, sanctification or bearing fruit is from the same Spirit who brings justification. Sanctification and justification are His products.

But the function of the believer is different in sanctified works. Regeneration, as noted above, is monergistic (i.e. the work of God alone, in which the regenerated person is passive). Although sanctification is also God's work, the believer is no longer passive but cooperative. However, just as our *faith* which brought justification did not merit justification, neither do our *works* which bring eternal life merit eternal life. The *Confession* avoids the Galatian error that Christians begin in the Spirit and finish in the flesh (3.1).

Finally it is evident that there is no justification apart from sanctification, or sanctification apart from justification. It is also equally obvious that there is no Jesus Christ as Savior who is not Lord, or Jesus Christ as personal Lord who is not personal savior. These are inseparably joined, and it is heresy to separate them.

16.3 Here the Westminster Assembly emphasizes what has already been stated in the preceding two sections and adds that the continuing influence of the Holy Spirit is necessary in believers, who are not, therefore, TO GROW SPIRITUALLY LAZY by waiting for the Spirit to do the work for them. This scotches any notion that the believer's "new nature" is a self-operating disposition, i.e. like a clock God winds up to work by itself thereafter. Any such deistic notion of sanctification was not in the Assembly's mind. On the other hand, pantheism is also ruled out. We do not "let ourselves go and so let God." "Quietism" is here quietly excluded as the Christian works out what God works in — but the believer must stir up the Holy Spirit in the first place.

Well, actually the *Confession* does not say "in the first place," but is it not implied? If Christians are not to be LAZY do-nothings and are "to be diligent in stirring up the grace of God that is in them" to do what only the Spirit can do in them, aren't they doing that much on their own? They are stirring up the Spirit. The order would seem to be: (1) Christians are to do *their* best; (2) they thus stir up the Holy Spirit; (3) He works in them to will and to do; and (4) they then do "good works." The Westminster Assembly might not agree to this list. They would probably call attention to the fact that they had said that Christians are not to wait on "a special motion of the Spirit." They would probably go on to argue that if the Christian did his best without the Spirit, his best would be altogether evil, and no Christian ever does an altogether evil deed. So what happens is that it is the Spirit who stirs up the saints to stir Him up! That is probably what they mean, and they are probably right.

16.4 At the Christians' very best THEY FALL SHORT. How true! In fact this section may contain the greatest understatement in the entire *Confession*. Why didn't they say that at their very best Christians fall *infinitely* short of their minimal duty? Why the anemic, THEY FALL SHORT OF MUCH WHICH THEY ARE BOUND TO DO? Their age probably could hardly bear as much as they did say. Our age rarely hears even that much truth.

They were also explicitly repudiating the accepted Roman Catholic doctrine of "works of supererogation." Before the Reformation, the Church had slipped so far from the true doctrine of "good works" that it actually taught that Christians are capable of, and often did, much more than they are bound to do. In such a context, the anemic understatement here does seem very bold.

How did the Roman Church ever fall into such depths of supererogation? They did so by confusing the objectively non-mandatory with a subjectively non-mandatory. That is, when they read that all men were not required to be "eunuchs for the kingdom" (Mt 19.12), they concluded that when some did become eunuchs for the kingdom, they went beyond what was required – they supererogated. What the Church overlooked was that *if* a man had that gift, he *was obliged* to serve God by using it, should the providential circumstances so indicate. For that particular subject of the kingdom, what was not mandatory for all was mandatory for him. His obeying was not *super*-erogation but a mere imperfect erogation.

16.5 It was said that Boston University's famous philosopher, Borden P. Bowne, not only annihilated his opponents in debate but dusted off the spots where they stood. Here the *Confession* is dusting off the spot where supererogationists once stood. So far from doing more than is required, men cannot "merit pardon." Christians can in no way pay or profit God, since they are still unprofitable servants, even defiling to a degree the good which the Spirit does within them.

Here any understatement in the preceding section is corrected. The real *Westminster Confession* stands up – and man, Christian man, has gone down. The Christian's works have gone down in significance in several steps. First is the GREAT DISPROPORTION between them and their works and any rewards. Next is the INFINITE DISTANCE between them and their God. They cannot profit Him. They cannot even pay for their own debts. WHEN (it should be "if") they have done all, it is only DUTY, and they are therefore UNPROFITABLE. The good they do comes from the Holy Spirit, anyway, and even it is DEFILED AND MIXED with their own imperfections. Therefore, by their best works, they only *deserve* damnation (judgment).

16.6 Jesus saves! Jesus saves! Not only sinners, but also believers, whose GOOD WORKS are ACCEPTED IN HIM and even rewarded in spite of all their WEAKNESS AND IMPER-FECTION.

If one began reading the *Confession* at this chapter and read this section, the reaction might well be outrage at what appears to be quintessentially moral favoritism. Only people who are BELIEVERS are treated as THOUGH THEY WERE PERFECT and accepted and rewarded for MUCH IMPERFECTION. How-ever, if we remember Chapter 8's detailing the wonderful redemptive work of the God-man mediator, expiating guilt, cleansing, and interceding, we can well understand the propriety and morality of this section.

We have a perfect example in the Garden of Gethsemane, where Christ took his three most intimate and beloved dis-ciples to watch with Him as He underwent His agony, sweating blood. Several times they fell asleep. What did He say to them? "The Spirit is willing, but the flesh is weak." You have disap-pointed me in your weakness, but I know you love me. The smoking flax Christ does not quench or break the bruised reed (Mt 12.20). So God, looking on the saved in His Son, IS PLEASED TO ACCEPT AND REWARD WHAT IS SINCERELY DONE, EVEN THOUGH ACCOMPANIED BY MUCH WEAK-NESS AND IMPERFECTION. Christians are made acceptable in the beloved (1 Pt 2.5).

16.7 Although as far as the deeds themselves are concerned, unregenerate men's actions may equal or sometimes even excel the moral deeds of Christians, yet, since these deeds are NOT DONE IN THE RIGHT WAY, they are therefore always sinful, i.e. incapable of pleasing God or even of disposing Him to give grace. Still, it is even worse for the unregenerate not to do these bad good works.

Notice that there are two aspects here: the content of the works, what is actually done, and their manner, how they are done. We usually speak of the outward and inward aspects or the objective and subjective. Whatever the language, the doctrine here is clear. Works of themselves may be good (honesty, for example, is virtuous or good) but not in their motivation (a person may be honest because "it pays" or seems to pay to be honest).

Sometimes the content of an act can cause us to mistake the manner. A man once ran into a burning building where two children were trapped and in danger of dying. A crowd outside shouted its approval for the man's heroism. When he came out of the building a few minutes later with a box of jewels and not the children, the crowd nearly killed him. Had he died in the flames, though, they would have erected a monument to his self-sacrifice!

Since good works must proceed from the God-man mediator, non-believers, therefore, never do a single good work in their entire lives. They may actually abound in apparent good works and, like Ghandi or Schweitzer, have monuments erected to their moral excellence.

Chapter 17

Concerning the Perseverance of God's People

The perseverance of the "saints" (GOD'S PEOPLE in the Summertown modernization) in Jesus Christ is a fact, not because of believers but because of: God and His decree; Christ and His intercession; the Spirit and His abiding; and the Covenant of Grace, which the Trinity has established for believers' salvation. Notwithstanding, the perseverance of the saints is not their perfection. It persists through grievous sins, divine discipline, and much misery to themselves and others.

17.1 Negatively stated, believers cannot fall away, and, positively stated, they will persevere to the end and be ETERNALLY SAVED. It might be asked whether they cannot fall away if they want to. The answer is, "yes, they could if they wanted to." To that answer there is a second question: "is the affirmation of that possibility not a denial of the perseverance of the saints?" The answer here is "no," and that precipitates a third question: "how can there be the perseverance of believers, if believers can stop persevering whenever they want to?" The answer, of course, is that they will never want to. They will *never* want to fall away.

Here it says that believers CAN NEVER COMPLETELY OR FINALLY FALL. As one great admirer of the *Westminster Confession* once said, "the saint [i.e. believer] may fall on deck, but he will never fall overboard." Greater than the Westminster divines, Calvin, Spurgeon, or any one or all of them, the word on which they all stood has it, "for a brief moment I forsook you, but with great compassion I will gather you" (Is 54.7). This is the final link in the golden chain that connects believers with the eternal decree and their final state in heaven.

17.2 The perseverance of believers is here seen to be the preservation of believers, not by their free will but by God's unchangeable love, Christ's inexhaustible merit, and the Spirit's eternal abiding—all according to the Covenant of Grace.

If one asks why the doctrine is called the *perseverance* rather than the *preservation* of believers, it is no doubt because believers do the persevering, while God does the preserving. But, if God did not preserve, they would not persevere.

All three persons of the Trinity are involved in the Covenant of Grace. God the Father does the choosing, the electing. Then there is the Son's unchangeable, sacrificial love, and finally the indwelling Spirit. These three activities establish the Covenant of Grace as the means of bringing believers by perseverance to eternal life.

17.3 In spite of their perseverance, believers may be troubled by their three traditional foes (the world, the flesh, and the devil) and by their own negligence in not using means against those foes, so that they fall into sin, grieve God, and hurt themselves as well as others, bringing on themselves temporal judgments. Some Christians deny the validity of the hymn's statement: "Prone to wander, Lord I feel it, wander from the God I love." The statement is indeed valid. Scripture teaches that corruption does remain in the best of Christians, whether they know it or not. The persevering of the saints depends entirely on the preserving grace of their God and Savior.

Literal "grieving" of the Spirit is, of course, impossible. He is God, and God's counsel stands fast. All is according to His eternal decree. He can never be frustrated so as to "grieve." However, He can and does show his hatred of sins, especially the sins of believers, in a way that men would consider evidence of His "grief." God is not a man that He should repent (Num 23.19), and so His "grief" is an anthropomorphic expression—an understanding of what God is like by drawing an analogy to man and expressing about God what would be thus expressed about man.

Now believers can have their HEARTS HARDENDED but not as Pharaoh's heart was hardened. Here is the difference. First Pharaoh's heart was never softened (although his resolution was), but a saint's always is. Secondly God ordained the hardening in Pharaoh's case to raise him up as a monument to God's holiness and wrath (Rom 9), while He ordains it for believers to bring them back to His love and favor. Therefore it is for judgment in the case of Pharaoh but for mercy in the case of believers. TEMPORAL JUDGMENTS are similarly means of grace and tend to promote eternal felicity as they call believers off from their sins and back to their God. "Thy rod and thy staff they comfort me."

From all this, anticipate, if you will, the next chapter on the assurance of salvation. What would the Westminster assembly come up with. The doctrine of election would tend to support assurance, but what about the imperfection of believers and their ability to commit serious sins? Do these two lines of thought tend to support or oppose a doctrine of assurance or call for some intermediate position such as outward certainty or preservation, but without inward certainty?

Chapter 18

Concerning the Assurance of Grace and Salvation

Four key things are said about assurance of salvation: (1) it is possible; (2) it is infallible; (3) it is non-essential; and (4) it can be lost.

18.1 Although assurance is possible, it is also possible for those who ought not to have it to have it. True regenerate believers, walking in love, may have it in this life and never be ashamed of it in the world to come. Note that since assurance of salvation is possible for the saved and unsaved alike, assurance *itself* would not seem to assure. That is, although you have assurance, your recognition that the unregenerate may also have it tends to make you unassured. But we are assured here in the *Confession* that Christians may be assured WITH CERTAINTY. How then can this assurance be certain, if the assurance itself may be either true or false? The answer is unfolded in the subsequent sections of this chapter.

It is interesting that historically speaking the doctrine of assurance has been a rare thing — not just for experience but also for theology. Even Augustine did not teach it, and Arminianism, which in one form or another has represented the majority view in the history of Christianity, cannot teach it. Although the Reformed tradition, of which the *Westminster Confession* is part, always teaches assurance, it does not nevertheless find it commonly experienced among its adherents. The Puritans (characterized, for example, in Jonathan Edwards) hedge about it with so many careful qualifications of the doctrine that it has been said that few of them were assured.

18.2 Assurance of salvation is infallible for four reasons. First it rests on infallible promises. Secondly the SPIRITUAL IN-SIGHT is given to us by God. Thirdly, we have the testimony of the Holy Spirit, and finally our spirits, along with His Spirit, testify also. Furthermore, the Spirit's presence also serves as a proof (seal) of our eternal redemption.

The crux of the whole matter is here in the infallibility of the assurance available to us. We not only can have assurance but an infallible assurance. Note that *implicitly* this section is saying that *all* Christians do have infallible assurance, unless, that is, some Christians do not have infallible promises, spiritual insight, and the testimony of the Holy Spirit and of their own spirits, as well as the presence of the Holy Spirit as a seal. Since, according to the *Confession*, those are the common possessions of all Christians, infallible assurance must also be the common possession of all Christians.

The *Confession* does not go ahead and recognize that implication, however, because of its position that assurance is *not* essential to faith — an apparent inconsistency, because if there is an INFALLIBLE ASSURANCE OF FAITH based on foundations common to all Christians, there seems to be no way that any Christian can be devoid of assurance. On the other hand assurance is clearly not essential to salvation and may be intermittent. The mistake here is failing to notice that it is not *assurance* that rests on these four foundations listed above, but *faith*. Assurance rests on faith, and faith may be weakened to the point of invisibility and assurance along with it.

18.3 This section makes clear that assurance is not essential to faith (and salvation) and that believers may have difficulty obtaining it. But assurance can be realized without a special revelation, and it is a duty to seek it diligently. Finally, when it is realized, the result will be a loving, thankful, strong, and cheerful obedience, rather than a presumptuous UNDIS-CIPLINED LIFE.

The main point here is that the foundations on which faith rests must be diligently sought in *experience,* if assurance is to be obtained. But, of course, the emphasis is also on the fact that the diligent search can be successful. Assurance may be achieved in this life. However, the implication is that, since it *may* be obtained, it conversely may also *not* be obtained. It may not be obtained even by Christians who do diligently seek it. But there is diligence involved in seeking assurance, and diligence results from *obtaining* it.

All of these observations are meant not only to show how to gain assurance of salvation and the blessedness of that experience but also to answer the majority of critics who deny its possibility or even its desirability, because they maintain that the doctrine of assurance only promotes apathy, smugness, and presumptuousness.

18.4 Difficult as assurance may be to obtain, it is not too difficult for it to be SHAKEN, LESSENED, OR INTERRUPTED from four specific causes: simple neglect; commission of SOME PARTICULAR SIN; SUDDEN OR STRONG TEMPTATION; or God's withdrawal of THE SENSE OF HIS PRESENCE. Nevertheless, the regenerate are never COMPLETELY without faith, love, and a sincere obedience by which assurance may be revived, and meanwhile they are always KEPT FROM COMPLETE DESPAIR.

Neglecting assurance obviously accompanies our neglect of other spiritual matters — neglect of our prayer life, of studying the Bible, of actively doing the things God expects and wants us to do. Frequently this neglect results in the committing of a particular, grievous sin, which separates us from God. Even sudden or severe temptation may unsettle our spiritual confidence. And, as a result of these and of any number of other sinful activities and attitudes and combinations thereof, God's chastisement may take the form of His withdrawing from us a sense of His presence. During that time, of course, all assurance of salvation will be correspondingly absent.

Chapter 19

Concerning the Law of God

The law is an expression of the character of God. It was first given in the form of the covenant of works. After the fall the moral requirements of this covenant took the form of the ten commandments, to which were later added the ceremonial and judicial laws (these latter EXPIRED with ancient Israel). The moral law in the Ten Commandments binds everyone, including those justified in Christ, who are under it, not as a covenant of works but as a conveyor of many benefits. And, of course, all uses of the law at all times comply beautifully with the grace of the gospel.

19.1 God gave the law to Adam, who was imbued with the power to keep it, and required him and all his descendants to keep it in order to continue life. Disobedience would bring death. This restatement of the covenant of works seems to project it beyond the event of its being disobeyed. The statement that God REQUIRED ADAM AND ALL HIS DESCENDANTS TO OBEY THIS LAW seems to imply that had Adam endured his probation obediently, the children who came after him would nonetheless have had the same terms of covenant still in force. And the requirement that it be obeyed PERPETUALLY also seems to imply that the covenant of works would be forever in force unless abrogated by disobedience.

However, the Westminster Assembly had a federal or representative view of the covenant with Adam (see 7.2), so that the reward of Adam's obedience, had he obeyed, would presumably have been his descendants' moral ability to keep the law without the possibility of sinning (*non posse peccare*). In the same way, Adam's disobedience, federally or representatively, incapacitated all his descendants, so that they do not naturally have the moral ability to obey God's law.

The intention here also seems to have been to reduce the operation of grace to a minimum in the covenant of works. Eternal life was not promised to Adam on condition of a period of obedience, but only moment-by-moment existence, until and if the covenant were to be broken. Still, even that is gracious, because, having done all, man really *deserves* nothing — not even continued existence for a moment. Man could have been annihilated without injustice, although, while still obedient, he could not have been punished without injustice.

19.2 Although as a covenant of works the law was abrogated by the fall, it continued as the PERFECT RULE OF RIGHTEOUSNESS and as such took the form of the decalogue. The moral law is never abolished but remains presumably for all time. The moral law given at Sinai then was the moral law of the Garden, less the stipulations of the covenant of works. So, it is essentially the same law delivered to God's redeemed people as was originally given to righteous and unredeemed Adam.

The moral law has two tables or divisions: that pertaining to God (one through four) and that pertaining to man (five through ten). In essence the moral law requires love of God, neighbor, and self (the law-keeper).

19.3 The CEREMONIAL LAWS were added to this moral law for the Old Testament church, prefiguring Jesus Christ. Therefore, they are now appropriately abrogated under the New Testament. If the moral law is a tutor to bring us to Christ, the ceremonial law shows us the Christ to whom the moral law brought us. Thus, under the Old Testament, Christ and Him crucified were preached and believed and worshiped. What John the Baptist did was to identify Jesus as the Lamb of God, prefigured, typified, and worshiped in the Old Testament church.

If Christ was typified, prefigured, and worshiped in the ceremonial law of the Old Testament, it follows that it was the church which worshiped Him. The very definiton of the Christian church is a company of believers in Jesus Christ. These Old Testament believers saw and worshiped Christ in their ceremonies, as the apostles saw and worshiped Him in His visible, incarnate presence. Christians today see and worship Him in and through the sacraments of baptism and communtion.

19.4 In addition to these CEREMONIAL LAWS for the church in her former state GOD ALSO GAVE THE ISRAELITES, AS A POLITICAL BODY, VARIOUS JUDICIAL LAWS. These traditional laws EXPIRED when that state of the church changed. While the moral law never changes, other laws not only change but actually EXPIRE. For example, the sixth commandment against killing remains, but the judicial law that *certain violators* of the moral law should be executed has not. Since capital punishment for such a violation as breaking the sabbath is not part of the moral law but only of the judicial, it EXPIRES with the end of the Israelite church-state.

However, capital punishment itself, for appropriate crimes, has not expired, because it is based on another Biblical principle, that of retributive justice (the *lex talionis*), which is permanent moral legislation, not enshrined in the decalogue, of course, but included in the provisions of the Noahic covenant (Genesis 9), which involves all humankind. If crime must be followed by punishment, then execution would seem to be the only fitting punishment for wilfull murder.

19.5 The moral law is perpetually binding on everyone, and the gospel, so far from cancelling that obligation, actually confirms it. The moral law has had its additions but never its subtractions, and never shall. Ceremonial and judicial laws may come and go, but the moral law, according to the *Confession,* abides FOREVER. Two reasons for this are here articulated. First of all the content of the moral law is a reflection and expression of the nature of its author, God. Secondly, adherence to the moral law is a necessary aspect of respect for such an author, God Himself.

This being the case, it follows that the Son of God would reaffirm the moral law, and any suggestion that He would do away with it in the gospel is actually unthinkable. Things have not turned out that way, of course. Doing away with the moral law has not been unthinkable, and even Christ Himself had to emphasize the fact that He came not to destroy the law but to fulfill it (Mt 5.17). Throughout the history of the church there has been a persistent tendency to misinterpret Romans 6.14, "we are not under the law but under grace," as removing the moral law from the realm of Christian duty (in spite of Christ's warning in Mt 5.17). Hence we have the grand conclusion of the *Confession* here: IN THE GOSPEL CHRIST DOES NOT IN ANY WAY REMOVE THIS OBLIGATION, BUT RATHER STRENGTHENS IT.

19.6 Building on that conclusion, this section explains exactly how the law serves the gospel: (1) as a rule of life, (2) by revealing the SINFUL POLLUTION in believers' lives and leading them to hate their sins, (3) by restraining Christians from their old sins, (4) by showing them WHAT THEIR SINS DESERVE, and (5) by revealing to them what blessings obedience brings. Nevertheless, this part importantly concludes, THE FACT THAT THE LAW ENCOURAGES DOING GOOD AND DISCOURAGES DOING EVIL DOES NOT MEAN THAT A PERSON WHO DOES GOOD AND REFRAINS FROM EVIL IS UNDER THE LAW AND NOT UNDER GRACE.

This section is the Psalm 119 of the *Westminster Confession* — a paean of praise for the law of God from a gracious heart. It was probably also the inspiration for Kevan's *The Grace of Law* (1963), a fine study of the Reformed view of the moral law. But the *Confession* makes plain that our great reverence for the perpetual obligation that Christians, as well as others, have to observe the moral law in no way is to be interpreted as a return to the Covenant of Works. The doctrine here is not a formula for salvation by works. A Christian must keep *all* of the moral law but is saved by *none* of it. And so the Westminster Assembly charts a careful course here between the Scylla of legalism and the Charybdis of antinomianism.

There are several ways to look at this. Christians are under the law, not as a meritorious basis for gaining eternal life but as a necessary life-style. And so the law no longer gives us a basis for experiencing the pollution of our natures but rather provides us with a way of hating sin and turning to the gospel to escape it. Similarly, the law is not the power restraining us from sin but rather points us to our need for Christ to restrain us from sin. The law does not make any satisfaction for our sins but shows us what we would deserve if Christ had not made satisfaction for us. Finally, the law does not bring us blessing but shows us the way we must behave in this life as the grace of God brings us eternal blessings.

19.7 The statement here merely concludes this grand chapter on the eternally grand LAW OF GOD.

Chapter 20

Concerning Christian Freedom and Freedom of Conscience

The original text has "liberty" for FREEDOM. Christian liberty includes the greatest freedom, from sin and death, plus free access to Christ's grace and life, further augmented under the New Testament. This liberty is in conscience to God. It is not to the illegitimate COMMANDMENTS OF MEN, not to mention the PRACTICE of SIN nor rebellion against ANY LAWFUL POWER, CIVIL OR ECCLESIASTICAL.

20.1 Christian liberty is exhaustively itemized here both positively and negatively. It includes: (a) freedom from the guilt of sin—but not from the power of sin; (b) freedom from the wrath of God—but not from the chastening of God; (c) freedom from the curse of the law—but not from the effects of the law; (d) freedom from the present evil world—but not from all its allurements; (e) freedom from bondage to Satan—but not from his ability to hinder and hurt; (f) freedom from the dominion of sin—but not from its rebellions; (g) freedom from the evil of afflictions—but not from the afflictions themselves; (h) freedom from the sting of death—but not from death itself; (i) freedom from the victory of the grave—but not from the grave; and (j) freedom from everlasting damnation—but not from temporal discipline. There is also the freedom to obey God, lovingly and willingly, without SLAVISH FEAR. All this and the New Testament, too, which includes: freedom from the ceremonial law; greater boldness of access to the throne of grace; and a fuller communication of the Spirit of God.

It should be noted that all these "freedoms from" have their qualifications. And, "freedom to" has its qualifications. This glorious loving obedience without SLAVISH FEAR does not mean that the liberated Christian never lapses into SLAVISH FEAR and always does give loving obedience. Finally and importantly, the difference between the New Testament believer and the Old Testament believer is one of degree not of kind.

The freedom from the ceremonial law is something which few Christians seem adequately to appreciate. Imagine having to slay thousands of animals, with all the blood and gore, as the very center of one's worship. We see now the utter necessity of it to grind into the consciousness of man that "without shedding of blood [there] is no remission" of sin, so that it would never be forgotten that the central significance of the Christian religion for eternity is the *blood of the Lamb of God*. Therefore Christians thank God for every one of those bloody sacrifices of old, and at the same time (now that they have learned their lesson in grace forever) thank Him that they can be free for all time from the gruesome laboratory of learning through which God put His ancient church.

Christian liberty not only allows a less gory religion but grants a much freer access to the God of all grace. The greater boldness comes from the fact that Christians see so clearly how the Lamb has taken away all their guilt forever and that nothing, but nothing, stands between them and God the Father. Old Testament believers knew this, too, but not so well as now, and they, therefore, had free but less free access to the throne of grace than Christians today.

Accompanying this is far greater inner freedom and boldness and far greater communications of the Holy Spirit Himself. It is the same glorious divine Third Person of the Trinity with whom Christians have to do as Old Testament believers had but with far more frequency, deeper intimacy, and more intensive and extensive influence among vastly greater numbers.

20.2 The phrase, GOD ALONE IS LORD OF THE CONSCIENCE, is probably the most quoted statement in the *Westminster Confession of Faith* and after the answer to the first question of the *Shorter Catechism* ("man's chief end is to glorify God and enjoy Him forever") the most quoted statement from the entire Westminster Standards. The statement deserves this prominence, because it refers to the most important of all human liberties, the liberty of conscience. From birth to death men are surrounded by authorities, but in and through all these human authorities there is no authority but that of God who ALONE IS LORD OF THE CONSCIENCE. Christians render no obedience to anyone except "in the Lord." Even if the authority itself be atheist with some legitimate authority over the Christian, obedience is rendered to that authority in the Lord and only in the Lord.

For this reason we have no supreme or ultimate loyalty to anyone except God. If our parents come between us and God, we are commanded by the Son of God to hate father and mother. And to hate Uncle Sam, also, if he ever tries to assert his authority over God's. We pledge allegiance to our nation only *under* God, never *above* Him.

20.3 The ugly head of Antinomianism is again beaten down here, as we are reminded that Christian liberty produces holiness rather than the practice of sin .

20.4 God intends church and state to be mutually supportive, so that opposition to THE LAWFUL EXERCISE OF POWER, WHETHER CIVIL OR ECCLESIASTICAL, actually amounts to RESISTING GOD, and such opposition should be PROCEEDED AGAINST BY THE CHURCH.

There is a significant change here in the American edition from the original section 4, which authorized not only the church but also the civil authorities to PROCEED AGAINST such opposition, i.e. the original *Confession* granted to the civil government certain authority in ecclesiastical affairs (of which more in Chapter 23). The original text reads: "they [i.e. those opposing THE LAWFUL EXERCISE OF POWER, WHETHER CIVIL OR ECCLESIASTICAL] may lawfully be called to account, and proceeded against, by the censures of the Church, and by the power of the civil magistrate." American Presbyterians excised the final phrase, "and by the power of the civil magistrate," leaving only the church to proceed against the ecclesiastically disobedient and disorderly.

The reason for this change is the disestablishment of the church in the constitutional organization of the United States in the 1780's. Since the government did not recognize an official church or Christianity officially, Thomas Jefferson's wall of separation between church and state went up. We are still wrestling with the implications of that separation today, since the United States' Constitution only forbids "a religious establishment."

In England the Anglican church and state are not separate. The monarch is the head of the state church, under God, and is, as well, the titular head of the state. The Westminster Standards were intended by Parliament to replace the Anglican state religion with its episcopal form (i.e. with bishops and priests) by a new, but more authentically apostolic (presbyterial) state religion.

This section then really does not make any statement about theocracy. The main point is that respect for government as government must be maintained by the church (not, however, governmental abuses of power) and that it is an ecclesiastical duty to proceed against those in the church who oppose legitimate civil power as well as ecclesiastical order.

Chapter 21

Concerning Religious Worship and the Sabbath Day

Although the "light of nature" or our NATURAL UNDER-STANDING teaches us that there is a God and that He is to be worshiped, only God's special revelation tells us how to do it. Everyone should engage in worship and prayer. Everyone should be prayed for except those who have committed the unpardonable sin. Worship services should include the reading of the Bible, sacraments, and other appropriate features. NATURAL UNDERSTANDING also teaches us that a particular time should be set aside for divine worship. Scripture specifies the Sabbath day, now the first day of the week, as that time. It is to be kept free from worldly activities and devoted to public worship, to private worship, and to duties of necessity and mercy.

21.1 This interesting section declares that men know God and the duty of worshiping Him from the "light of nature" but can only properly worship Him according to the "light" of Scripture. This declaration follows naturally from the declaration in 1.1 that human beings naturally know that God exists. It logically follows that if men know there is a God who is responsible for their being and their preservation, then it stands to reason that they should worship Him. Men do not need special revelation to teach them the obvious.

So, no special revelation is needed to teach men that they should worship God, but it is needed to teach them how. The logic is inevitable here, too, since it follows that, if God does tell His creatures how to worship Him, that is certainly the way, and the only way, they should do it. It also follows that if the worship prescribed by Scripture is the only acceptable way, then all other forms of worship are unacceptable and objectionable— NEITHER THE IMAGINATIONS AND DEVICES OF MEN NOR THE SUGGESTIONS OF SATAN ARE TO BE FOLLOWED.

It would not, however, logically follow that men must not, therefore, worship God by ANY VISIBLE REPRESENTATION. The divines probably should have stated here that we are not to worship God in such a way because God Himself forbids the use of images in worship.

21.2 Three prescriptions about worship are laid down here: (1) only the triune God is to be worshiped; (2) no creature and nothing else are ever to be worshiped; and (3) since the fall of man, acceptable worship *must* involve the mediation of Christ.

At one stroke this brief section rules out all worship by non-Christians, by Christians using human intermediaries (e.g. Roman Catholics), and even by Protestants who fail to name Jesus Christ as divine Mediator of their worship. There was a storm of protest in this country and throughout the world in the eighties when a Southern Baptist minister was quoted as asserting that Jews could not acceptably worship God, because they did not do so through Jesus Christ. The *Westminster Confession* agrees completely with that pastor and condemns all those who condemn him, especially fellow Christians and fellow Baptists. "There is *one* mediator between God and man, the man Christ Jesus" (1 Tm 2.5).

This section also shows us that "divine worship" is not necessarily good or even necessarily divine worship. According to the *Confession*, God does not accept, indeed deplores, worship not addressed to Him as triune, in the name of Jesus and according to the teaching of His word. Jesus remarks that even though the Pharisee who went up to the temple to pray uttered words addressed to the deity he did not succeed in praying to God; he only "prayed thus to himself" (Lk 18.11).

We are often called on to "respect" other people's worship and prayer. But how can we respect what is disrespectable?

There is a way. The expression means that we should respect the legal *right* of a person to "worship" as he pleases. As Americans, we do respect that political *right*, but we do not respect the divine right of what God Himself condemns. We will let our friends know that we sadly respect their right to go to hell in their own way. Anything less than this betrays a certain lack of concern for our friends, even when concerned with defending their liberty.

21.3 God requires everyone to pray, but acceptable prayer is only to be made through Christ by the help of the Spirit in a known tongue. There is a theological Catch-22. All men, regardless of their faith or lack of it, are required to offer thankful prayer to God. But, if they are not Christians, their prayers do not meet the requirement. The prayers of the wicked are an abomination to the Lord (Prv 28.9). So, men are required to do what they cannot do without conversion. What is the conclusion? All men must meet divine requirements. In their present sinful state, they cannot meet this divine requirement. Therefore they must be converted. But of themselves they cannot be converted. Therefore they must seek the Lord while He may be found (Is 55.6), and, if they find Him, they will meet the requirement of thankful prayer. If not, to all their other sins will be added this sin of omission (of proper, thankful prayer).

Authentic prayer is beautifully triune: (1) offered to God (the Father especially); (2) in the name of Jesus the Son; (3) BY THE HELP OF THE SPIRIT. The Spirit inclines us to pray to the Father through the mediation of the Son.

Another essential part of acceptable prayer is that it be ACCORDING TO HIS WILL. This means His will as revealed in Scripture. In other words, prayer must be according to the directions in the Bible. Otherwise, it is what in Colossians is called human "will worship" (AV 2.23).

But where does the person doing the praying come in? With the UNDERSTANDING, REVERENCE, HUMILITY, FERVOR, FAITH, LOVE, AND PERSEVERANCE. Not only is the divine obligation to pray important but so is the *way* of prayer to him or her who prays. We must be extremely careful. One cannot pray to an unknown God, but neither can one pray to the known god without true humility and other appropriate attitudes. Non-Christians obviously cannot (or should not) pray, except in penitence. It is equally obvious that Christians must not pray irreverently, without perseverance, etc.

Finally, it would seem to go without saying that a minister cannot lead a congregation which does not understand Latin in a Latin prayer. The *Confession* says it anyway.

21.4 The objects of prayer are anything and everything LAWFUL as well as all living persons, except those who HAVE COMMITTED THE SIN UNTO DEATH.

The LAWFUL THINGS here has a catch. We may ask for anything lawful, *if* it be God's will to grant it. We may pray to find a new job, the right school, to have good health, and the like, *if* it be God's will. We do not want these things, or should not, if they are not according to His will. We do not pray that God would go against His infinitely better judgment. We want His judgment to prevail. So, we do not ask for good health or life itself (as Hezekiah foolishly did) unless it is His will. That is the only way we could pray in His name, i.e. according to His character of sovereign wisdom. The Christian takes comfort in the fact that God will answer us "above all we can ask or think" (Eph 3.20).

There is also a difference between prayer for things and prayer for qualities such as love, joy, and peace. We do not ask for the latter conditionally, "if it be your will," because God has already told us that it is His will for us to have those qualities. Indeed, He commands such virtues.

As for other people, we may pray for those who are dead in their sins (except the unpardonable sin) but not for the dead. Once they are dead, people are gone from our world of experience. We have no active communion even with dead saints, not to mention dead sinners. Prayer for the dead, therefore, is dead prayer.

But what about prayer for the conversion of those we know who are dead in their sins? Is that prayer conditional or unconditional? It must be and obviously is conditional prayer, because God has never promised us to convert everyone, not even everyone for whom Christians pray. George Mueller and many other Christians have prayed for the conversion of some people for decades, sometimes without these people ever coming to the Lord and being saved. In these instances we must say with Christ, " I thank thee, O Father, Lord of heaven and earth, because thou hast hid these things from the wise and prudent, and hast revealed them unto babes . . . for so it seemed good in thy sight" (Mt 11.25-26).

21.5 Religious worship is divided into two parts: (1) ordinary worship, which includes: (a) reading Scripture, (b) sound preaching, (c) conscientious hearing, (d) Psalm singing (with grace in the heart), and (e) sacraments (properly administered); and (2) special worship, which includes: (a) religious oaths, (b) vows, (c) fasting, and (d) thanksgiving.

Scripture, of course, is the foundation of worship. It is to be read with reverence and heard conscientiously. SOUND PREACHING here means orthodox exposition of the Bible. This is what was done in the seventeenth and eighteenth centuries. We are usually far from it today. In fact a recent review of fifty outstanding contemporary sermons revealed that not even one of them was a serious exposition of Scripture. Much was to be learned about contemporary affairs and leading political figures but next to nothing about the Bible and even Jesus Christ.

Conscientiousness is important here. The requirement for CONSCIENTIOUS HEARING OF THE WORD would seem to exclude non-Christian visitors. Unless a person is converted, he cannot be truly conscientious, especially in relationship to the Bible as the word of God. But, of course, unless he hears the word, he will never be converted and become conscientious. We should probably conclude then that the Westminster divines mean conscientiously as far as an unconverted hearer may be conscientious (see Rom 2.14-16).

The singing of Psalms has also now just about died out. Originally Reformed churches only allowed congregational singing of the Psalms, because they were authentically and authoritatively Biblical and hence lacked the potential contamination of false teaching which might come from the mere human authorship of hymns. Subsequently, however, hymns (which are not even mentioned by the *Confession*) have been introduced into Reformed liturgical use and have virtually driven out what is mentioned and was once exclusively sung.

This section also provides for special services, which are enumerated, although only thanksgiving services are common today.

21.6 The scope of worship is covered in this section. Although worship is not now restricted to a particular place, it is to be public, private, and in families.

After David and before Christ, Jerusalem was the appointed center of worship and could not legitimately be disregarded. In the gospel age, no *particular* location is sacred, but we may not therefore conclude that *some* place is unnecessary. Since public worship is necessary, it is also necessary for God's people regularly to worship God at an agreed place.

Church attendance is not optional but necessary. It is sometimes said that Roman Catholics go to church because they have to and that Protestants go because they want to. In fact, however, if we perform a duty merely because we want to, we are not really doing our duty.

The *Confession* points out that it is also an obligation to worship regularly in the family and privately by ourselves. Since all three are indeed commanded in Scripture, a Christian is not worshiping the triune God aright, if he is not worshiping Him in the three places: heart, hearth, and church.

21.7 Nature teaches that some time should be given to the worship of God, and Scripture tells us which time: one day out of every seven. At first that day was the seventh day, celebrating the creation of the world. From now until the end of this age it is the first day of the week, celebrating Christ's re-creation of the world through redemption.

There is no *essential* change in the Sabbath principle by changing the day from the seventh to the first. The proportion remains the same, and the decalogue is not altered. Seventh Day Adventists err, of course, if they argue otherwise. If it is once admitted that the change could take place without altering the Sabbath concept, then the fact that Christ rose on the first day, appeared on the first day, ordered His people to assemble on the first day, appeared to John for the final revelation on the first day, should be evidence enough that it has changed. There is no essential change then except the day, and this in effect perpetually continues the *Sabbath day*.

21.8 Here is the Puritan Sabbath in its purity. After preparing for the Sabbath BEFOREHAND, the whole time is to be taken up in public and private exercise of worship except for works of necessity and mercy. *All* worldly employments and *recreations* are to be put aside.

Since the Sabbath day is to be set aside, preparation for that day should not be on that day. The cattle have to be in the barn before the Sabbath begins, not afterwards.

There is to be a holy rest *from* the secular as well as rest *in* the sacred. And not only is there to be rest of body but from WORDS and THOUGHTS as well as WORKS. Not only must a Christian desist from unnecessary work on the Sabbath, but unnecessary talking and even thinking about work. This rest also includes rest from RECREATIONS. Thus the Sabbath rest described here is based on a different concept from the very common view, which considers recreation itself as rest from work. According to the *Confession* Christians should rest from that kind of rest, too, on the Sabbath.

The whole time and not merely part of the morning is to be given over to the duties of the Sabbath. For many Christians who attend morning worship services on Sunday the commandment to keep the Sabbath day holy has become, "remember the Sabbath hour to keep it holy."

That "Christ is Lord of the Sabbath" (Lk 6.5) is sometimes construed as meaning that the Sabbath has been eliminated. But the verse in fact is a confirmation of the Sabbath. If Jesus is Lord of the Sabbath, and He is the one who gave it, and He has never changed its duty, then it is still the same and involves the same moral obligations as when He gave it.

Another passage which is sometimes similarly misconstrued, "the Sabbath was made for man, not man for the Sabbath" (Mk 2.27), is also a confirmation of the Sabbath law, not an excuse for disregarding it. Christ is simply assuring us in this passage that the Sabbath, the whole seventh day, was made for the benefit of man. All its requirements, privileges, and restrictions are divinely beneficial for man, not a tedious chore.

Works of MERCY hardly need illustration—Christ Himself gave them (healing a man and rescuing an animal) — but works of NECESSITY may. Necessary does not mean convenient or preferable but inevitable for a moral existence. Thus a necessary work is probably not going to be one necessary to keep your job, but that your job is necessary to human existence. And so, hospital work is necessary on the Sabbath, but catching up on your office or school paperwork is not.

The original Sabbath celebrates the creation of the world. The new form of the Christian Sabbath celebrates the new creation of the same world. The old world and old Sabbath were made for man. The new world and the new Sabbath are made especially for the new man.

Chapter 22

Concerning Lawful Oaths and Vows

Lawful oaths and vows are acts of RELIGIOUS WORSHIP in the name of God, according to the New Testament (as well as the Old), committing one only to what is good and made in language which is understandable and clearly establishes the obligation to anyone. They are to be performed religiously for the purposes of: duty, thanksgiving, or obtaining something. Such oaths bind oneself MORE STRICTLY but never to anything: which is forbidden, which hinders doing one's duty, or which is beyond one's power to fulfill. Monastic vows are examples. Far from being works of supererogation (i.e. going beyond one's duty) they are actually works of superstition and are downright sinful.

Many Old Testament passages are cited in this chapter to show that God not only permits but requires oaths. Obviously, also, in the opinion of the Westminster divines the New Testament does not teach otherwise. So, swearing by the Word of God is taught by the Word of God. The "swear not" of Jesus (Mt 5.34) refers to swearing vainly by anything *other than* the name of God not to swearing by His name.

Yes, a person must always tell the truth whether he swears by the name of God, but swearing adds conscious solemnity for the swearer and assurance of veracity to those before whom the oath is taken. The rationale is, of course, the assumption that no one in his right mind would wilfully call down the judgment of God upon himself and therefore must be telling the truth.

But what about those who swear in God's name who do not believe in God? They cannot meaningfully do so, of course, but, if hypocritically they do, they are asking for divine judgment on themselves.

22.1 Lawful oaths are defined by the intervention of two divine operations. First God is called on to witness the truth of what is asserted. Secondly He is called on to judge the one who makes the assertion.

22.2 This section brings the solemn oath down to earth in the courtroom. Since to swear vainly is indeed a great sin, the magistrate wisely tries to assure truthfulness by requiring oaths, while Christians have an obligation to offer them. Since oaths were justified by Old and (implicitly) New Testaments, they are valid today and to be honored in courts of law--revealing the enduring character of Biblical prescriptions, unless explicitly changed.

Note the implication here that Quakers and others who will not swear oaths, because they understand the Bible to forbid taking oaths, have unenlightened consciences. The *Confession* does not say whether unenlightened consciences should be obeyed or not. Note too that since oaths and vows are so solemn, they ought to concern only IMPORTANT MATTERS.

22.3 Since oaths are so solemn, they must be considered carefully before being taken, and then they must be made only after one is COMPLETELY CONVINCED something is true. Even then he who takes the oath cannot be bound to sin, although it is a sin not to take a necessary moral vow when REQUIRED BY LAWFUL AUTHORITY.

It is, of course, never legitimate to sin, even if one has solemnly sworn to do so. He has already sinned in swearing to carry out something which would be a sin. He is not permitted to sin further by carrying it out, but to acknowledge his sin in making the promise in the first place, explaining that he was COMPLETELY CONVINCED the vow was right and true when he made it.

If it is a sin to make the wrong vow, it is also a sin not to make the necessary and right one. So the Quakers, by implication, sin in refusing to take a legitimate vow required by the magistrate, or, just as a Presbyterian would sin in taking a vow that he cannot fulfill for natural or moral reasons.

22.4 This section explains that vows are to be taken honestly, according to the general understanding of the terms used, without inner reservations, and are to be carried out at any cost short of sin. If the previous section may seem to take exception to Quakers, this one unquestionably attacks Jesuits, who were infamous, even among fellow Roman Catholics, for EQUIVOCATION AND MENTAL RESERVATION. Jesuit intentionalism allowed a person to intend something other than the words were generally understood to mean, without explaining his double-talk. According to many Roman Catholics and all Protestants, this was a violation of truth and did not "provide things honest in the sight of all men" (Rom 12.17).

MENTAL RESERVATION, another favorite of the Jesuit casuists, allowed a person to admit he stole the rope without mentioning that there was a horse tied to it. Not false, but the MENTAL RESERVATION would be, shall we say, misleading? Or, saying that the new baby was the most beautiful you had ever seen (mental reservation adding "today"!), or when an unwelcome visitor arrives, having the maid say that you are not at home (meaning not at home to him). According to the *Confession* these are not lawful statements.

Once taken, a vow must be discharged, no matter how costly, if it is not sinful to do so. A plumber once promised solemnly that he would do a $40 job on a certain Monday morning. He never showed up. If he had had to pass up a $4,000 job for his services on the condition that he start on that same Monday morning, he would have been morally obligated to forfeit that larger order in order to do the smaller one he had sworn to do—i.e. unless he had been released from his promise. Of course, plumbers are not the only ones held to their vows, nor do they have any particular professional propensity to break them. But it is extremely common for people to break their promises if fulfilling them works out to their disadvantage.

22.5 The essential difference between a vow and an oath is that the former is not necessary but is entirely optional. We are under a religious obligation to take some oaths (e.g. in court), but there is never any obligation to make a vow. That is completely up to the individual. The *Confession* says nothing, of course, about "resolutions," and probably would regard them as mere good intentions to which a person does not bind himself by sacred commitment. But one should probably not even make resolutions without serious intention to fulfill them. New Year's resolutions that are usually made in order to be broken are hardly moral ideals.

Although private and made with God alone, a vow is nevertheless utterly binding, once it has been made. Vows are a recognized means of grace little used now, and little use is indeed better than light use, but neither are as good as sacred use. There used to be a church in Philadelphia called the Vow Church, because a man built it who had made a vow when the ship in which he was crossing the Atlantic was in danger of sinking. His vow was that if he ever arrived on dry ground, he would build that church.

We should also remember that since vows are optional, they cannot legitimately be made about a duty which is obligatory. One cannot make a sacred vow to be honest or not to steal anymore, for example, because we are all under a divine obligation to be honest. Making such a vow, insults God by implying that only when someone voluntarily puts himself under a vow is even a divine obligation binding.

22.6 This section seems to suggest just that sort of problem described in the preceding paragraph. Here a vow is said to be aimed at thanks for the past or requests for the future with two realms of application: NECESSARY DUTIES and OTHER THINGS. But we cannot really make a vow concerning NECESSARY DUTIES. Anything that is necessary is so by virtue of a divine requirement, the basis of all morality. The obligation is total and allows of no excuses. We do not, therefore, understand how the *Westminster Confession* could say that A VOW BINDS US MORE STRICTLY TO NECESSARY DUTIES. How can one be bound more strictly than by a command of God?

Can a voluntarily assumed obligation be more binding that a divine prescription?

It is, of course, easy to understand how this phrasing came about. We all recognize how far short of the glory of God we constantly fall. In penitence we ask for forgiveness and resolve not to repeat the shortcoming. Ashamed of our shortcomings, we want to be especially resolute to overcome them and would do everything possible to fortify ourselves for the future. Thus, we are inclined to make an additional solemn promise. We can understand this, but we really don't see how it can be justified. Divine commandment is for nothing short of perfection. We are under constant obligation, constant divine obligation. There is simply no way we can oblige ourselves more strictly than we are already obliged. God is certainly pleased with our penitence and our asking for divine grace to fulfill our duties and not fail in them, but He probably does not appreciate our imagining that we bind ourselves to those duties more than He has already bound us.

There is a modern example of this in the rather common practice of married couples repeating their vows. Again, it is easy to understand why people would be tempted to do that. Nevertheless, they are perfectly obliged by their initial vows to be faithful unto death. It is impossible for them to be any more strictly obligated than they have become by their initial vows. If, somehow or other, by doing that they can examine their lives and endeavor to observe their faults and correct them, that is all highly desirable. But it is probably not desirable to suppose that a renewal of vows binds the parties more strictly to their duties than they have been bound by prior obligations laid upon them by the divine commandment about marriage.

22.7 Since vows are optional and can only be made concerning things which are capable of being performed, and since monastic vows violate this principle, they are not a means of grace but an occasion of sin. A man or woman simply does not know whether he or she has the gift of continency for life and therefore cannot promise to remain unmarried. Protestants have sometimes taken similar vows, but in so doing they are under the same indictment. One may well vow that as long as he/she does have that gift, he/she will abstain from marriage. However, an unqualified vow, as is required in monasticism, allows no such exception and is itself therefore sinful rather than an aid to virtue. This is not to say that a person making such a vow does not often successfully perform it. But no one knows at the time whether he will be able to and therefore cannot vow to abstain from marriage, which has as one of its purposes to avoid fornication. Such a vow is indeed a SINFUL TRAP from which a person certainly must extricate himself.

Note that this indictment of monasticism includes the related sin of requiring celibacy as a condition of ordination.

Chapter 23

Concerning Civil Authorities

The present form of this important statement on church and state reflects significant modification of section 3 made by American Presbyterians in the 18th century to lessen the authority of the civil government over matters of religion, but it still (a) sees God as the supreme head appointing civil authorities as His subordinates whom citizens are to obey and (b) gives the civil authorities the responsibility of protecting the church without the right of intervening in ecclesiastical affairs or abridging church government. The pope is explicitly denied any civil authority or authority over secular government.

23.1 God ordains and uses the civil authorities to encourage the good and punish the evil (THE POWER OF THE SWORD). Christianity, of course, is a religion of authority with God as the ultimate authority from whom the civil government derives its authority. There is no divine authority, however, for the civil authority to do as it pleases or to violate moral principles.

23.2 Since civil government is itself from God, Christians may lawfully hold office and participate in that government. When so involved in civil authority, they are, however, to be sure to support TRUE RELIGION, JUSTICE, AND PEACE. They may also lawfully WAGE WAR ON JUST AND NECESSARY OC-CASIONS.

In the seventeenth century the Anabaptists were the most prominent opponents of Christian participation in government, holding that serving in public office or in the military were essentially serving in the devil's uniform. Here the *Confession* takes the usual, orthodox position that public and military service are appropriate exercises of Christian responsibility.

The Summertown editors have rendered TRUE RELIGION for the original's "piety," assuming, probably correctly, that the Westminster divines intended that only orthodox Christianity deserved to be supported and maintained by the civil authorities, Christian or otherwise. The 18th-century American revisers probably construed "piety" in a broader, more liberal way which would tolerate the heterodox along with orthodoxy.

But no reading of this section will allow the civil authorities to administer unbiblical laws — presenting an interesting dilemma for Christians participating in government, particularly in our own, very secular age which is moving farther and farther away from Biblical positions, e.g. on divorce and homosexuality.

In the 17th century the question of pacifism was probably a bigger problem than it is now, at least among Christians. The pacifists did not usually deny that warfare was lawful according to the Old Testament. The *Confession* asserts here that it is also lawful in the New and cites four proof texts, all from the New Testament (Lk 3.14, Rom 13.4, Mt 8.9-10, and Rv 17.14,16). However, this right to wage war is restricted to JUST AND NECESSARY OCCASIONS. And so, only on moral occasions may a government wage war.

23.3 This section has been radically altered by 18th-century American Presbyterians. In the original the civil authorities are ultimately responsible as overseers for the proper organization, administration, worship, and teachings of the church. They are explicitly, for example, to ensure "that all blasphemies and heresies be suppressed." In this way the Westminster Assembly simply replaced one state church (the Anglican) with another one (the Presbyterian). The poet Milton, a true nonconformist, complained bitterly of this action in a famous 20-line sonnet, "On the New Forcers of Conscience [i.e. the Westminster divines] under the Long Parliament," which concludes with a scathing pun based on the fact that the words presbyter [of the new Presbyterian regime] and priest [of the Anglican Church] have their etymological origins in the same Greek word: "*New Presbyter* is but *Old Priest* writ Large."

The American modification here is quite different. The civil authorities must merely PROTECT not oversee THE CHURCH OF OUR LORD, allowing freedom for all denominational interpretations and beliefs and even guaranteeing that all people, Christian or not, shall be protected from religious persecution or abuse. The government is also to guarantee the freedom of assembly of all religious groups.

There does seem to be a distinction here, though, between the true church of Jesus Christ and other religious groups. While the civil government is TO PROTECT THE CHURCH OF OUR LORD, it is apparently not bound to protect other churches and religious organizations, but only the people in them from religious persecution, that is, every PERSON, religious or not, is to be protected but the only organization to be protected is the Christian church. Religious liberty then is allocated to all only after a fashion, while governmental protection is to be given only to orthodox Christian denominations.

23.4 Whatever the civil government may be and no matter whether its officials are Christians or not, it is the duty of Christian citizens to pray for it and obey its every lawful command, including the payment of taxes. The pope has NO POWER OR JURISDICTION in this relational scheme and particularly has no authority to administer capital punishment against heretics. The Assembly probably thought this point needed specifying in an age when Catholics made a practice of executing heretics (as, of course, a few Protestants did). It should be noted that although the original wording of this section does not explicitly extend the power of capital punishment to the civil authorities' responsibility to suppress ALL BLASPHEMIES AND HERESIES, such authorization is certainly implied by THE POWER OF THE SWORD in section 1. American toleration of different religious beliefs (including heresies and atheism) has probably come to a much better position in the 18th-century American revisions reflected in this section as it now stands.

Although the pope is only mentioned in the second part of this section, Roman Catholic positions are actually being opposed in both. The Roman church does not officially recognize authority not approved by the church. But, according to the *Confession* Christians must acknowledge and pray even for those civil authorities who may be opposed to Christian beliefs.

There is still another point here related to Roman Catholicism, according to which the pope does have authority over the civil government as well as the church. No civil authority can legitimately rule without papal permission. The famous two-swords theory maintained that the pope wields spiritual power directly through the church and civil power indirectly through the civil government. Here the *Confession* denies that extension of authority into civil affairs.

Chapter 24

Concerning Marriage and Divorce

There are three chapters on marriage. The original was discarded and rewritten independently by both the PCUSA and the PCUS in the twentieth century.

The original chapter teaches monogamy as the Christian doctrine of marriage with four purposes: mutual help, offspring, a HOLY SEED for the church, and prevention of adultery. Consequently it is lawful for everyone to marry, although Christians must marry other Christians. Another qualifying restriction is provided by the Biblical laws of consanguinity (which was abbreviated in paragraph 4 by American Presbyterians). Adultery justifies but does not require dissolution of the contract, as does willful and irremediable desertion, and the innocent may remarry.

24.1 Marriage is between one man and one woman. Polygamy and polyandry are forbidden, as are, of course, on these as well as other moral grounds, any and all perverted relationships between men or between women.

24.2 Four reasons are given here for marriage. There seems to be no particular significance in their order, except that MUTUAL HELP is appropriately put before procreation. The Bible states that it was "not good for man to be alone" (Gn 2.18). While classifying the various animals, Adam saw their existence in pairs and sensed his own insufficiency and incompleteness. That is the Biblical account of the existence of the female: for a necessary companionship, including but comprehending far more than sexual companionship. Recognizing the mutual help and identity of being, the *Confession* is true here to

Genesis 1.25, where it states that God created man, male and female, from the very beginning. The account of woman being formed from man, therefore, means distinguished or separated from him, bone of his bone, flesh of his flesh. So companionship was built into the creation of Genesis 1 and spelled out in the distinct creation of woman in Genesis 2.

The second reason for marriage, PROPAGATION OF MANKIND, is a result of the mutual, sexual helpfulness of the man and woman. This sexual helpfulness is the basis of propagation and therefore more fundamental than propagation. That this procreation among Christians involves RAISING UP OF A HOLY SEED obviously means at the very minimum that children should be reared in the nurture and admonition of the Lord and should be considered a "holy seed" while being so raised. Whether more than this is implied is taken up in the later chapter on baptism (28).

Marriage is also a means of avoiding disgrace. The natural appetite for sex, given as it is by God, often cannot be restrained. Marriage is then the legitimate, godly outlet. Better marry than burn, Paul observes (1 Cor 7.9). This does not imply that all who marry do so only for that reason. However, that is an honorable and just reason for marriage. Involved in this reason is the corollary that neither husband nor wife is to deprive each other sexually (1Cor 7.3-5). Adhering to this God-given and immensely practical command would prevent so many problems which occur among married couples, as the Roman Church, with its doctrine of the debt of the body, has taught for hundreds of years.

24.3 Marriage is honorable and lawful for everyone with the exceptions implied and listed here. The first implication is that those who are mentally, emotionally, or physically unfit may not marry. The second is that Christians should marry only fellow Christians. The *Confession* then explicitly excludes non-believers: Roman Catholics, adherents of other idolatrous relgions, the notoriously wicked, and heretics, as unfit for the Christian to marry. Violation of this command, however, does not nullify such marriages with unbelievers.

The universality of marriage would seem to deny that the church should require an ecclesciastical ceremony even for its own members. This institution is an instance of the common grace of God and subject to the law of God and the state which He appoints.

While it may be legal for a Christian to marry anyone otherwise fit, believers are duty bound TO MARRY ONLY IN THE LORD. It may be *legal* then to marry someone other than a fellow believer but it is at the same time *sinful.* Believers are limited here to non-Catholics and even, apparently, to Reformed Protestants. The Westminster divines did not accept the Roman use of images or her doctrine of transubstantiation as anything other than idolatry. The bracketing of Catholics with INFIDELS also indicates that the Reformers viewed Catholic theology as unsound as the mass. Intermarriage could therefore never have the blessing of the Reformed church.

The separate listing of the NOTORIOUSLY WICKED and heretics may point to professing Protestants whose lives or some of whose doctrines are markedly contrary to sound practice and thought.

24.4 Biblical laws of consanguinity must, of course, also be observed. Although the American version of the *Confession* drops some of the specific details from this section, its utter repudiation of this kind of marriage is unchanged. Adultery does not necessarily dissolve a marriage, but violation of consanguinity nullifies it. Adultery seems even to destroy marital legality. If so, here is a case where the church asserts her authority above the state, if the state allows such marriages. The case of Henry VIII and Catherine of Aragon may well have been on the Assembly's mind. Catherine had been married to Henry's older brother, Arthur, before marrying Henry, who in turn used the Biblical laws of consanguinity to have Arthur's marriage annulled as incestuous after they had been married for twenty-four years and had had six children.

24.5 Adultery after marriage legitimates the dissolution of the marriage contract by the innocent party and his or her remarriage. It need not do so, but it may. The innocent party *must* forgive and *may* be reconciled to the continuance of the marriage. It is a duty to pardon but not to resume the marriage. The guilty party is DEAD so far as the marriage is concerned, and the innocent party may regard him or her as such or may resurrect him or her, as it were, as a living and continuing partner.

Since the guilty partner is DEAD to the marriage, the innocent one is free to divorce and remarry. Although marriage should not be rent asunder, it may be rent asunder and a new marriage legitimately formed by the one not responsible for its ruin. A spouse is forbidden to rend asunder, but if he does, according to the Westminster divines, the other spouse is free to form another marriage. Just as natural death legitimately dissolves marriage, so its equivalent of moral death does the same and entitles the bereaved to marry again. When the spouse does not take this option, it implicitly amounts to the innocent spouse's second marriage to the same person

Roman Catholicism errs to the right and much contemporary Protestantism to the left of this doctrine. Rome will allow no legal divorce with the right to remarry. Many modern Protestants allow divorce and remarriage on many other than the two legitimate grounds. Such is the confusion of our time that many Roman Catholics are far to the left of center and some Protestants, who deny any remarriage regardless of the grounds for divorce, far to the right.

24.6 Condemning what Presbyterians were later to do, the Westminster divines and their early American counterparts warned agains the CORRUPT NATURE OF MAN that is inclined to loosen the strict marriage-divorce laws of Scripture. The *Confession* specifically limits the just grounds for divorce to adultery and irremediable desertion only. At the same time it insists that divorce procedures must be PUBLIC AND ORDERLY. Note that the CORRUPT NATURE OF MAN seems to include the remaining corrupt nature, even of regenerate man, because these unapproved divorces seemingly are prevailing in the professing church today. As we will see when we come to these modern changes, this corrupt nature operates and is justified under the rubric of the "spirit of the Christ or Christianity."

After the attention to adultery earlier, this section also adds DELIBERATE DESERTION WHICH CANNOT BE REMEDIED as a legitimate ground for divorce. No particular time limit is set, although it would seem that some considerable time would have to pass to prove that desertion is irremediable. Even if the departing spouse says that there never would be any reconciliation, some time would have to pass before that assertion could be taken as final.

Chapter 24

Of Marriage and Divorce (PCUSA)

The Presbyterian Church in the United States of America rewrote this chapter in the twentieth century. The changes are significant mainly for what is omitted. What is affirmed is really not out of accord with the original chapter.

24.1 Absent here is a full list of the purposes of marriage along with any reference to prohibitions against violations of consanguinity or even unequal marriages between believers and nonbelievers.

24.2 Here the deviation from the original is positive. Remarriage is allowed after a divorce on grounds "implicit in the gospel of Christ" and when accompanied by penitence. What is implicit in the gospel of Christ must then be determined according to the judgment of the church and not by any *necessary* implication of Scripture. This new determination has opened a Pandora's box of virtually promiscuous divorces. Adultery and desertion are no longer necessary or the only grounds, which have become in this view anything thought by the church to be consistent with the gospel.

Chapter 24

Of Marriage and Divorce (PCUS)

The Presbyterian Church in the United States also effected an independent revision of this chapter. The first two paragraphs duplicate the first two paragraphs of 'the original, but what follows involves considerable alteration. The changes include: dropping reference to the Reformed faith as a requirement for both parties in a Christian marriage; dropping sexual activity and infidelity outside of marriage as the explicit grounds for divorce; the guilty partner is no longer considered legally and maritally dead; only "irremediable unfaithfulness" allows divorce to be "considered;" divorce is allowed, not because God's word allows it but because the church judges a spouse's "failure" to justify it; and remarriage is allowed "when sufficient penitence for sin and failure is evident" (i.e. evident in the view of the church) – not when, as Christ allows, the non-guilty partner has been freed to divorce and remarry.

24.3 Now a marriage with non-Christians is not strictly forbidden, although such a union cannot be "fully and securely Christian in spirit or in purpose." And the original's prohibition against Reformed and Evangelical Christians marrying the non-Reformed and non-Evangelical is now changed into the milder encouragement for Evangelical Christians to "seek as partners in marriage only persons who hold in common a sound basis of evangelical faith."

24.4 This new paragraph would be quite compatible with the teaching of the original were it clearly a reference to the marriage of Christians. But such a limitation is not stated or clearly implied. The significance of the church wedding is apparently to show the religious significance of marriage, but at the same time it is not specified that the partners in marriage need be religious at all. Furthermore, this section ends with the promise of "God's grace within [the couple's] new relationship," even though, as far as this provision indicates, they need not even be Christians.

24.5 Here again is significant change, mainly from the traditional grounds for legitimate divorce and remarriage. We have seen that the original form of the *Confession* allows only adultery and irremediable desertion as legitimate Biblical grounds for divorce and the right of the innocent party to remarry. Not only is such a statement missing here, but what is stated is both more vague and far more inclusive. The "weaknesses" of a married couple may be such that the union becomes "intolerable" — presumably becoming the legitimate grounds for divorce and remarriage of either divorced partner. This statement is immediately qualified, however, by the limitation that "only in cases of extreme, unrepented-of, and irremediable unfaithfulness (physical or spiritual) should separation or divorce be considered." Neither the Bible nor the original give such limitations, which are then confused by their applicability only to the *consideration*, not the act itself, of divorce.

The final sentence in this paragraph reveals the real break with the original: "Such separation or divorce is accepted as permissible only because of the failure of one or both of the partners, and does not lessen in any way the divine intention for indissoluble union." It is the undefined "failure" that allows the dissolution of the marriage. That failure is not defined so as explicitly to include the two failures of Scripture, adultery and desertion, or to exclude any other (conceivable to the mind of the church) failures. One can sense here a tendency to return to the Roman position of absolute indissolubility. Nevertheless, such is not said or implied. There is no question, of course, that the divine intention is the indissolubility of the marriage relationship. Nor is there any question that God does not permit the dissolution of that relationship, except on His own specified grounds of adultery and desertion (according to the mind of the original *Westminster Confession*). What the revision does here is in one sense to narrow the divine statement, as if God did not permit divorce at all on any grounds, and at the same time actually to open up the possibilities of divorce to an unlimited number of grounds which could qualify in the *church's* opinion for the designation, "failure."

24.6 The statement here is in open defiance of Jesus Christ's teaching in Matthew 5.32 and 19.9, where it is unequivocally stated that whoever puts away wife or husband "except for fornication" (*porneia*, i.e. any and all sexual activity outside of the legitimate union of marriage) and marries another commits adultery and may become the occasion of the innocent committing adultery. In sharp, rebellious disobedience to the teaching of Christ, our revisers remark that "the remarriage of divorced persons may be sanctioned by the church, in keeping with the redemptive gospel of Christ, when sufficient penitence for sin and failure is evident . . .." Christ never indicates any such allowance, "in keeping with the redemptive gospel of Christ."

24.7 We need not comment on this particular piece of ecclesiastical reflection except to say that it seems to be a gratuitous addition taking itself more seriously than the words of our Lord and His Scripture.

Chapter 25

Concerning the Church

The true or invisible church consists of the elect of all ages and times, but her visible form is made up of those who profess true religion and their children. Using the ordinances given by Christ for the gathering and perfecting of regenerate believers, the visible church is the means of salvation. Although never perfect, some visible churches always exist but some of them become so impure as to *cease* being churches. Christ is the only head of the church, and the pope, so far from being the head, is in fact the Antichrist.

25.1 The most important statement of this important chapter here identifies and defines the church as invisible. Invisibility is not merely an aspect of the church, it is the church's essential nature – at least for the present. Note that the *Confession* includes among the elect those who WILL BE GATHERED in the future (i.e. at any one point in time). Essential to Roman Catholicism is the visibility of the church, with the pope as visible head. Essential to Protestantism is the invisible church, with its invisible head, Christ. The invisible church is universal with the implication that no church, Roman or other, is *the* church, precisely because all these churches are visible. All Reformed churches are, of course, also visible, but, as we shall see in the next section, visibility is not their essence.

In light of the relation of the church to Christ is there any propriety or validity to the common contemporary expression of the "continuing incarnation of Christ?" Or, to put it another way, is there a continuing hypostatic union – i.e. is the divine person of Christ the person of the Church? To put it this way enables us to see the blasphemy of the common assertion. So, the question becomes: is that the only meaning of the "continuing incarnation of Christ?" There seems to be no other valid interpretation of such language, and the notion should therefore be rejected with horror. The church does not fill all in all. Rather she is the spouse and body of Him who does fill all in all. Note that, in the same way, Christ's human nature did not fill all in all, even though it was and is the body of Him who does fill all in all.

25.2 The visible church in the world consists of all who PROFESS THE TRUE RELIGION along with their children and is therefore the universal kingdom of the Lord Jesus Christ by which everyone is ORDINARILY saved. There are two aspects of the church, invisibility and visibility. In one are all the elect, whether converted or not or even existing or not (at any particular time). In the other, the visible church, are only those who profess faith and their children — although not everyone in the visible church is in the invisible church and not everyone in the invisible church is in the visible. Subsequent sections elaborate and explain this situation: of the church as invisible and visible; of the true church and the mixed; and of the body of Christ differing from the kingdom of Christ.

The visible church is called universal, because it is no longer limited or confined to Israel but is worldwide. This was anticipated in Old Testament times when some gentiles were converted and brought into the Israelite church. Now the church is so universal that it is the believing Israelites who are brought into the gentile church.

Notice that the principle of *extra ecclesiam nulla salus est* (outside of the church no one is saved) has an absolutely necessary qualification. The principle properly refers to the invisible church and asserts the proposition that no one can be saved except in the invisible church.

The *Westminster Confession* not only differs in its identification of the visible church as Protestant rather than Roman Catholic but differs also in its evaluation of the true, visible church. It, too, believes that the church is a *Heilsanstalt*, an institution for salvation, but not, however, an indispensable one. As we have seen earlier, God's Spirit works when, where, and how He pleases. Although He pleases ORDINARILY to work through the visible church when He brings anyone into salvation, i.e. into the invisible church, He does not always or necessarily do so. This is the reason baptism for the Protestant church is *evangelically* but not *absolutely* necessary, while, according to Roman Catholicism, it is not merely evangelically but absolutely necessary.

25.3 The *Confession* continues to focus here on the visible church, observing that the ministry, Scripture, ordinances, and Spirit are given to her according to Christ's promises. The visible church then is the means for the gathering and perfecting of the invisible church — i.e. the visible church exists for the sake of the invisible church. Hence the emphasis here on the visible church, although the less important of the two aspects of the church.

There is also the inevitable merging of the invisible and visible churches. The invisible church is gathered into the visible, and so the invisible church tends to become the visible church — or the invisibility takes on visibility. It is easy then to see how Roman Catholicism was tempted (and succumbed) to identify the two. The connection is very close and *ideally* is complete — i.e. the ones who respond to the ministry, Scripture, and ordinances of the true visible church would normally be the elect or the members of the invisible church. Finally all the means of grace, ministry, Scripture, and ordinances are given not only to the invisible but to the visible church as well.

25.4 Not only is there a difference between the invisible and visible churches, there are also, as here, vast differences of degree among the visible churches in their particular bodies according to the varying purity of their administration of the means of grace and their actual PUBLIC WORSHIP. Although the next section will point out that these differences sometimes reach the vanishing point, here the lesson is that the visible church is never itself pure but always MORE OR LESS PURE.

In evaluating PARTICULAR CHURCHES then, one must consider the various ordinances and the responses to and effect of them. The purer the ordinances, i.e. the more closely tied to and reflecting Biblical truth, and the more exact the response to them in worship, the purer that part of the visible church. A visible church, therefore, is not to be judged by its size, money, success, or program, but by its means of grace and the use thereof.

25.5 Three points are made here about the visible church. First, no chuch is perfectly pure. Second, some churches are so impure as not to be churches, and third, there will never be a time when all visible churches have become that impure — i.e. there will always be some imperfectly pure churches.

No church, just as no member, will ever reach perfection in this world. It goes without the *Confession* saying, that all visible churches, as all visible Christians, should strive for perfection, although neither ever achieve it UNDER or before HEAVEN. It follows that visible Christians should be associated with the most pure visible churches, and both should help each other strive for perfection. Choosing a church is not then merely a question of proximity or some other worldly consideration.

It is also clear that a visible church may cease to exist. It may continue to claim to be a visible church, when it is in fact no more. If the best of visible churches are subject to impurity and error, the worst of churches have ceased to be altogether. Since this sad possibility is true, we are warned not to believe everything churches may tell us. Not only read the label, but examine the contents as well.

In our opinion the majority of once visible churches are now visible churches in claim only. Such churches are SYNAGOGUES OF SATAN, an expression from Revelation 2.9. Although they claim to be true churches, they actually belong to the devil and not to Jesus Christ. The major synagogue or synagogues of Satan will be identified in the next section. Before we turn to that, we are encouraged by the assurance that never will the time come when all churches are non-churches or SYNAGOGUES OF SATAN. Divine providence will see to it that THERE WILL ALWAYS BE A CHURCH ON EARTH TO WORSHIP GOD ACCORDING TO HIS WILL. Christ asks whether the Son of Man will find faith on earth when He returns (Lk 18.8)? The *Confession* answers: "yes, there will always be at least some churches and some Christians waiting for Him."

25.6 Finally we see that the apparently visible church claims two heads: Jesus Christ and the anti-Christ or pope of Rome. This strong statement about Roman Catholicism cannot simply be dismissed as historically conditioned by the violent religious differences of seventeenth-century Europe. The visible church, as truly as the invisible one, has only one Head, the Lord Jesus Christ. If it denies that one true Head, it ceases to be a visible church. So the visible church has an invisible Head who is head of both churches, invisible and visible.

Rome's error is in making the invisible head of the church visible in the so-called Vicar of Christ, the pope. Since Christ has not abdicated His throne, the pope is guilty of usurpation. Although invisible, Christ is not absent and does not need a visible presence to avoid absence. He is personally and really present, as the acting Head of His body, the church, even in its visible form. Following 2 Thessalonians 2.3-4, the *Confession* therefore charges the pope with glorifying HIMSELF AS OPPOSED TO CHRIST and God, because he does not submit to that headship but thrusts his own head in its place — thereby becoming the anti-Christ, which leads Jonathan Edwards to call Romanism "Satan's masterpiece" (*Works*, I, 595)

Although the definite identification of the anti-Christ seemed clear enough at the time of the Westminster Assembly, any study of Evangelical and Reformed commentaries which have been written on 2 Thessalonians, 1 John, and Revelation during this century will demonstrate a wide range of proposed identifications among Protestant exegetes, who continue to wrestle with this point.

Chapter 26

Concerning the Fellowship of God's People

All the elect are united with Christ and with one another in Him. Therefore we are obliged to help one another in every way and everywhere, not only by spiritual communion and worship but also in "outward things" (26.2). However, this communion does not make believers partakers either of Christ's deity or of their fellow Christians' property.

26.1 Here is the general statement of Christian communion with Christ and with one another in gifts and graces. The most important point is that believers are united with Jesus Christ in all His grace, suffering, and exaltation. *En Christo* is a key doctrine of the New Testament and of the *Westminster Confession*. This union is the basis of, the ground for, and the incentive to the union of believers with one another.

The same fellowship which God's people have with Christ they have with each other—as in His graces and gifts, so in their graces and gifts. The way they participate in graces and gifts is different, of course. Grace is the grace of Christ, the common divine source from which all believers draw. He gives each his portion of grace and gifts which follow, and these directly enrich the whole body of Christ. Thus, Christians are to share with other Christians whatever Christ has given them individually.

This sharing is both spiritual and physical, or inward and outward. We communicate our knowledge and experience of the word and Spirit so as to provoke fellow believers to good works (Heb 10.24), and we distribute our worldly goods to meet their physical or outward needs. One does not have one without the other: grace without willingness to give gifts (Jas 2).

26.2 Here it is plain that the communion of the saints (FELLOWSHIP OF GOD'S PEOPLE) involves spiritual and material things and includes not only members of one's own church but of other churches as well. This section is more specific and more comprehensive than the first section, while it leaves limitations on these obligations for section 3.

Christians are committed to help each other spiritually. One does not merely join a church but joins a working-together fellowship where each part is to minister to the spiritual well-being of every other part. Those who are received into fellowship, no less than those who receive, become instantly one spiritual family, loving one another and helping one another better to serve their common Lord and Savior, Jesus Christ.

These helps extend to material things, because Christians are material as well as spiritual beings. Christ's redemption is for body and soul, saving body as well as soul. It does so partly by the help that His members give each other, body and soul. Christian man is a body/soul and so shall this ministry be to both.

This section also takes notice of the body catholic or universal. The visible church is catholic as well as particular, and each of these must be concerned with the other in both kinds of needs. Christ's visible as well as His spiritual body aims to be one, universal, and catholic and must act accordingly. If a person is concerned only for himself and not his fellow church member, or if a church member is concerned for his particular church and not the church catholic, he is neither a catholic nor a true Christian.

26.3 Now come the limitations of this union, which, however penetrating and pervasive, are not all inclusive. Specifically, this union does not include the deity of Christ, nor all the possessions of His members. Communionism is not communism.

It seems incredible that any professing Christian would ever imagine that his union with the divine Christ acutally includes possessing His deity. But this heresy has appeared. Sometimes it is stated or sung without, hopefully, being realized. Thus one of the church's hymns says, "Make me like Thee, divine" — a blasphemous request for deification, which actually appears to be worse than the unpardonable sin. That sin attributes the *work* of the Holy Spirit of God to the devil, while this claims the *person* of the Son of God for oneself. The great difference is, presumably, that while the committers of the unpardonable sin know what they are doing, these others would be horrified if they did.

Sometimes this form of impiety and blasphemy takes a more obscure form not so easily detected. The formula, "let go and let God," does not claim deity for the Christian who "lets go," but it does plead for God to be his life rather than himself, and that is quite blasphemous, although probably rarely so intended. But even if unintended, it ought nonetheless to be corrected. We ought not for centuries to give currency to such slogans. Paul was crucified with Christ, and Christ lived *in* Paul, but not *instead of* Paul.

There is also the tendency, less serious but not insignificant, for men to appropriate their fellow Christian's property in the name of the fellowship of believers. The *Confession*'s opposition to such communism implies that the obligation one Christian has to share his property with a needy brother is to be determined by the one who has and not the one who has not. Certainly the temptation would be for the needy to claim common possession more than for the rich to pool all. Those who "have" then must be aware of those who "have not" and of the obligation they have to alleviate the needs of fellow Christians. The degree to which one should bring himself down and his needy brother up is a matter of private, personal judgment. We must each answer to Christ for our stewardship and assume the responsibility for not giving too little or giving too much.

The early church experiment in Christian communism seems never to have been mandatory or continued, although some

Christian groups ever since have repeated the same experiment, with, of course, repeated lack of success. Nevertheless, *true* Christian communism as defined above is simply the life of the Christian church.

Chapter 27

Concerning the Sacraments

Sacraments are signs and seals of grace, which serve four purposes: (1) to represent Christ, (2) to confirm receivers of Christ, (3) to distinguish these receivers from non-receivers, and (4) to engage receivers in the service of Christ. Since there is a spiritual union of the sign and what is signified by the sign, the terms are used interchangeably. The actual power of the sacraments does not come from themselves or the one administering them but from the Spirit of God to worthy receivers. There are only two sacraments, baptism and the Lord's Supper, which are the same in substance as the Old Testament sacraments.

27.1 This section outlines the four purposes listed above which explain the institution of the sacraments as signs and seals of the Covenant of Grace. The sacraments represent the meaning of the Covenant of Grace (Christ for believers) and seal or confirm that relationship to worthy recipients. Whatever vast differences may obtain among churches concerning the sacraments, it is interesting that these two are invariably recognized (however many more) and that they are acknowledged as signs and seals (whatever further significance may be added).

The first and third and fourth of the purposes are easily understood, but the second is not immediately obvious. How exactly do the sacraments CONFIRM OUR POSITION WITH AND IN HIM? The sacraments are tangible signs of the reality of God's uniting us to Himself in His Son. From this perspective, baptism is the sacrament of our once-for-all union with Christ (as in Romans 6, we are baptized into his death and resurrection), and communion is the sacrament of our continuous union with Christ and our renewal more and more into His image. But does the *Confession* mean here that the sacraments establish our relationship to Christ as the Roman Catholic doctrine of *ex opere operato* teaches? Any such notion is repudiated later in this chapter. What then is meant? The point seems to be this. If our relationship with Christ is what the sacraments represent, they become a visible confirmation of that fact. The sacraments endorse a relationship that already exists, *if* it does exist. Confirmation does not bring it about, if it is *not* there prior to the administration. This will become clearer as we proceed through these chapters on the sacraments.

The third purpose, TO DEMONSTRATE A VISIBLE DIFFERENCE between recipients and non-recipients is obvious, of course, and not very important in a Christian nation, but it is extremely important in a non-Christian or anti-Christian nation or culture. Once one has received the sign of baptism and it becomes known, his separation from the rest of his culture cannot be denied, and often ostracism or persecution follows. This fact tempts many to avoid the sacraments or receive them secretly and call themselves "secret believers."

27.2 Since there is a SACRAMENTAL UNION between the sign and the thing signified, THE NAMES AND EFFECTS OF THE ONE ARE ATTRIBUTED TO THE OTHER. God's sacramental action means that He takes up into His power a material element which He unites for a time with the divine element (the activity of God's Spirit) so that the entire event effectively conveys the grace which is pictured in the material sign. As Calvin says: "in the sacraments the reality is given along with the sign" (*Commentary on Isaiah* 6.7).

The Westminster divines certainly followed Calvin on the reality of sacramental union. Calvin asserts that God would never hold forth "an empty symbol" (*Institutes* IV.17.10). Sacramental action means that believers do not go through an empty ceremony but "are given the thing itself" (Calvin, *Commentary on Acts* 22.16). This means that God graciously works along with the human activity mandated by Scripture to convey His grace to those who exercise faith.

There is an analogy here to the union of the two natures in Christ. Christ's two natures, divine and human, are united in one person. Consequently, the name and effects of the one are attributed to the other (or, more precisely, the activities of each nature are attributed to the One Person of Christ). An example of this is the expression, "blood of God" (Acts 20.28). Blood is a possession only of the human nature, but because of the union of the human nature with the divine, it is attributed to the divine Person. With the SACRAMENTAL UNION, the sign, water, is united with the thing signified, spiritual cleansing. So, we have the expression, "born of water" (Jn 3.5), where birth refers to the new spiritual birth and is attributed to the physical sign, water. Water does not cleanse spiritually or bring regeneration. The heresy of baptismal regeneration, however, comes right out of this confusion of sign and thing signified.

In reality then the sacrament does not work *ex opere operato* or mechanically accomplish what it signifies. Rather, there is a SACRAMENTAL UNION, which, although it is real insofar as it is used by the Spirit of God as He chooses to convey grace to hearts of faith, is certainly not a magical or automatic physical union between the two, under human or ecclesiastical control, as was erroneously imagined in the medieval church of Rome.

But if the sacramental union is not a magical or automatic physical reality, the question then arises whether the sacrament and its union with the thing signified has any value. Let us remember Calvin's position, quoted earlier, that, for the true believer, in the sacraments we have "no bare figure, but the giving of the thing itself" (*Commentary on Acts* 22.16). But we can easily understand how appealing the doctrine of *ex opere operato* is and why it has been so widespread and so comforting to some who receive sacraments. Truly error is often easier to understand than truth.

27.3 This section simply affirms that the efficacy of the sacraments does not come from the sacraments themselves per se or from those who administer them. Efficacy comes only through and by the Holy Spirit fulfilling the establishment of them and the promises about them in the Bible.

27.4 Here it is asserted that THERE ARE ONLY TWO SACRAMENTS and that they may be administered only by ORDAINED MINISTERS.

27.5 The Old Testament circumcision is the New Testament baptism (Rom 4.11 and Col 2.11), and the Old Testament passover is the New Testament Lord's Supper (1 Cor 5.7). These REVEAL IN SUBSTANCE THE SAME SPIRITUAL THINGS.

Chapter 28

Concerning Baptism

Baptism has the characteristics of a sacrament already described and specifically is a sign and seal, UNTIL THE END OF THE WORLD, of: (1) THE COVENANT OF GRACE, (2) THE BELIEVER'S INGRAFTING INTO CHRIST, (3) REBIRTH, (4) REMISSION OF SINS, and (5) YIELDING TO GOD TO WALK IN NEWNESS OF LIFE. Using water and the triune name, a minister sprinkles infants of believing parents. Although required, baptism is not absolutely necessary for salvation. As for efficacy, THE GRACE PROMISED IN IT IS NOT ONLY OFFERED BUT ACTUALLY EMBODIED AND CONFERRED BY THE HOLY SPIRIT TO EVERYONE (ADULT OR INFANT) TO WHOM THAT GRACE IS GIVEN, ACCORDING TO THE PURPOSE OF GOD'S OWN WILL AND IN HIS APPOINTED TIME.

28.1 Here is the listing of the five benefits (enumerated above) signified and sealed by baptism. It is easy to understand how baptism signifies the Covenant of Grace, the ingrafting into Christ, rebirth, remission of sins, and the believer's walk. But how does it seal them? Certainly the human sacramental action alone is insufficient to accomplish this spiritual sealing. Otherwise everyone baptized is elect and/or will be regenerate. The Westminster divines believed no such thing. What then does the sealing mean? It means that whatever is pledged will be completely fulfilled. Sacramental sealing then is like the relationship between the two natures of Christ—the human and the divine are neither confused (i.e. the sacrament does not replace the sovereign working of the Spirit of God) nor separated (i.e. the human aspects of the sacrament are not empty of spiritual blessings to faithful receivers of them). Baptism seals or confirms the fact that the water does signify these things. In other words, sealing is a divine stamp of approval on baptism as a sign. So it is not a mere sign thought up by men, but ordained by God with His official stamp of approval. That much, no more, no less, seems to be meant.

The assertion that baptism is to be CONTINUED IN CHRIST'S CHURCH UNTIL THE END OF THE WORLD refutes Quakers and any others who spiritualize the sacrament or in any other way render it obsolete. Evangelicals sometimes do the same thing by asking to be baptized again, if they think they were not Christians when first baptized — thus implying that the sign and seal are of no validity unless accompanied by an inward experience corresponding to the symbolism.

28.2 Proper baptism involves: plain water, no oil; in the name of the triune God, not in the name of the Son only; and administration by an ordained minister, not just anyone. Although baptism may not be saving in itself, it still must be performed if at all possible and performed properly. That much is essential to salvation. There is no efficacy in the rite itself, but there is infinite efficacy in the person who commands it. If we desire His power, we will obey His commandments. In the day of His power, the people shall be willing (Ps 110.3) to be baptized according to His will.

Baptism is to be administered by A LAWFULLY CALLED MINISTER. A mature Christian man, long ago baptized, as he thought, realized that he had never been baptized at all. How so? There had been a ceremony, and there was water. But it had not been in the name of the triune God nor by a proper minister. He had been baptized in a Unitarian church by a Unitarian minister, and a false church has no true LAWFULLY CALLED MINISTERS. He therefore arranged to be baptized in his trinitarian church by a proper minister. Conversely, baptism performed by a liberal minister, but in a trinitarian church, is valid baptism. The efficacy of the sacraments, as noted previously, does not depend on the state of the minister's heart.

28.3 The proper mode of baptism is sprinkling. Dipping or immersion is unnecessary but not forbidden. The *Confession* believes that the word for baptism in the New Testament neither signifies nor forbids immersion. There is no cavalier spirit here. What God commands must be treated with utter seriousness and sincerity. The Westminster divines and others argued that God has not required immersion, and some have even argued that He actually requires sprinkling.

The argument is too complicated to review here. However, the fact that the creed does not forbid immersion seems to imply that that mode is not impermissible. Baptists do not usually think the same about the reverse position but suppose that the Greek *baptizo* does require immersion and nothing else. Some baptistic groups consider a person unbaptized, if not immersed, and unsaved, if not baptized. The question for them becomes whether (assuming sprinkling to be incorrect) it is possible for fellow Christians to be sincerely in error? If they cannot be, then they cannot be Christians.

This is a problem for Baptists to wrestle with and for any Christians to wrestle with anywhere that there is a difference of opinion about the commandments of God's word. Does the error admit of the possibility of a person being Christian who makes it? In that case, one should suppose that he may be a Christian because his error is not fatal or quintessential. This is the way those of the Westminster position feel about necessary immersionists, because they consider the error non-fatal. But Christians may not and cannot feel the same way about Unitarians who deny the deity of Christ, because the Unitarians deny what no one can deny and still be a Christian. How can a person be a Christian without Christ? And how can Christ be Christ without His deity?

28.4 Here infant baptism is declared to be the teaching of the Bible. No argument is given, and we cannot develop one except to say that it grows out of the fundamental doctrine of the continuity of the Covenant of Grace in the Old and New Testaments—a doctrine frequently expressed in the *Confession*. If the people of God are the same in both dispensations, and the sacraments the same in substance, then the children included in the Old Testament by right of circumcision, are certainly not excluded in the New Testament from the equivalent right of baptism. In fact, the greater richness of the New Testament is shown by the rite of baptism, which includes female children as well as male.

There is probably no area of Reformed theology--pedobaptistic Reformed theology — where there is greater division. The three common views are: (1) all baptized children are elect and regenerated at some time or another; (2) should they die before the age of accountability, all baptized children are thereby shown to be and to have been regenerated; (3) all baptized children are not necessarily elect, but some are, and there is a great hope and even probability that baptized children reared faithfully in the nurture and admonition of the Lord will be brought to the Lord savingly.

28.5 One may be lost with baptism and saved without it, but it is a great sin to condemn or even neglect it. These implicit principles are made explicit here. Obviously, if Christ instituted this rite, it is not to be condemned or neglected. But if the sign and seal are outward and not necessarily inward, then not all are saved who are baptized. Furthermore, since the Holy Spirit works where, when, and how He pleases, He not only can but may regenerate persons without sacraments as He sometimes does without the word.

This is sometimes called the doctrine of the *evangelical* necessity of the sacrament as distinguished from the *absolute* necessity. The difference is that the absolute necessity of the sacrament means that a person cannot be saved without the sacrament. Augustine (unfortunately) believed this, and here official Romanism agrees with him where it should not, just as it usually does not agree with him where it should.

Evangelical necessity is the doctrine that once something is commanded, it must be obeyed, and refusal to do so, when possible, is a refusal to obey Christ — and such obedience is absolutely necessary to salvation. Baptism is not absolutely necessary per se to salvation, but obedience to Jesus Christ is. If a person realizes that Christ has commanded baptism, it is, therefore necessary for him to be baptized, and not to be baptized under such circumstances, is a deliberate policy of disobedience, which shows that person not to be a Christian.

This then is the basis for the *Confession*'s conclusion that ONE CAN BE SAVED AND REBORN WITHOUT BAPTISM, AND, ON THE OTHER HAND, EVERYONE WHO IS BAPTIZED IS NOT THEREFORE UNQUESTIONABLY REBORN.

28.6 The efficacy of baptism, when it is efficacious, is not TIED to the moment of baptism, but it is CONFERRED to the elect at the APPOINTED TIME. This is the Reformed equivalent of baptismal regeneration. Although no magic is involved, of course, grace is CONFERRED at the time of baptism, and regeneration will occur at the APPOINTED TIME in those for whom God intends it, i.e. the elect.

The *Confession* is always careful about covenant implications. Just as it says concerning baptized infants dying in infancy that SOME are elect and ventures no further, so it is equally cautious in this section. The truism in the doctrine of election is that the elect will be saved at the APPOINTED TIME, whenever that may be. So, the *Confession* here says that the elect baptized in infancy will have CONFERRED grace that will be made effectual at the APPOINTED TIME (before, during, or after baptism).

28.7 It is universally accepted that baptism is to be administered only once. You may object that pedobaptists (infant baptizers) call the other baptists, anabaptists (those who baptize again). We so denominate them because, in our opinion, they do baptize a second time. But how then can you say that baptists who baptize twice agree with you about baptizing once? We can call them double baptizers because, not admitting infant baptism, they baptize again on profession of faith. But they do not consider infant baptism to be baptism. They do not consider people who have been baptized as infants to have been baptized at all, and so they consider people who are baptized along with their profession of faith to have been baptized for the first time, no matter whether they were baptized previously as infants or not.

They say then that we infant-baptizers do not baptize at all, and we say that they baptize twice. But we all agree that we all should baptize only once; at least once, but never twice.

Chapter 29

Concerning the Lord's Supper

The Lord's Supper was instituted by Christ for these purposes benefitting HIS MYSTICAL BODY: (1) remembering his sacrifice, (2) sealing His benefits, (3) spiritual nourishment, (4) engagement to all duties, (5) the union and pleasure of that union with Christ and fellow believers. It is a "spiritual oblation" (which makes the Roman Catholic sacrifice of the mass "abominably injurious") to be administered by Christ's ministers only to those "present in the congregation." Such practices as private masses, denial of the cup, or worship of the elements (the bread and wine) are forbidden, and although called by the names of the things they represent, the elements remain what they are, bread and wine. WORTHY RECEIVERS do not carnally but spiritually receive Christ and the benefits of His death, while the IGNORANT and WICKED (unworthy partakers) receive nothing but "their own damnation."

29.1 The first section lists the five benefits for believers from this sacrament. Although all five are easily understood, it must be remembered, as is stated later, that these benefits only come to those who are WORTHY RECEIVERS. There is, of course, no actual masticating of the body of Jesus and drinking of his blood. This is a spiritual transaction benefitting only spiritual partakers.

We might well call this sacrament the nourishment sacrament, just as baptism is the initiation sacrament. Baptism signifies and seals the beginning of life, while the Lord's Supper involves the nourishment for the continuation of this new life into eternal life. As Jesus Himself said, unless you "eat my body and drink my blood, you have no life in yourselves" (Jn 6.54).

29.2 This sacrament does not re-sacrifice Christ but rather commemorates His once-for-all sacrifice and is a spiritual not a fleshly or carnal offering. Consequently the Roman Catholic version of this sacrament DOES DETESTABLE INJUSTICE to the one and only sacrifice and propitiation of Christ. Commemoration is absolutely crucial here, because there is and has been only one sacrifice. Commemoration therefore always declares that fact and precludes any misunderstanding that there is a repetition of Christ's sacrifice, while the Roman Catholic mass actually teaches that pernicious doctrine.

Now it is true that many modern Roman Catholic theologians have attempted to explain their "sacrifice of the mass" as not a sacrifice of the mass but a commemoration. However, as long as it is called a sacrifice and not a mere commemoration, no amount of effort at interpreting it as a commemoration will avail. If there is but one sacrifice of Christ on the cross of Calvary, there simply cannot be millions of others on thousands of altars. If Rome is truly ashamed of her teaching, as she should be, let her repudiate the language by which it is taught rather than try to have non-Romanists understand it as compatible with sound doctrine.

Another great Reformed creed, the Heidelberg Catechism of 1563, calls the Roman sacrifice of the mass, "abominable idolatry." These condemnations by Westminster and Heidelberg are really understatements of the seriousness of this crime against the cross of Jesus. If the sacrifice of Christ has to be repeated, its infinite value is implicitly denied, and that is not only a detestable but an infinite *injustice* to the true value of the blood of Christ, the God-man.

29.3 The administration of the Lord's Supper must be in accord with the meaning of it, as it is here described. The minister's partaking shows that he is a dependent recipient as well as an administrator. There is no essential difference between him and those to whom he administers, as there was between Christ and those to whom He administered. Christ did not receive; He only gave. Those who belong to Christ do not give; they only receive. And it is Christ who gives through them.

The Westminster divines insist that the sacrament should be administered only to those present in the congregation, just as Christ gave the first Lord's Supper only to those present when it was first instituted. The Lord's Supper was given for Christ's body, which is the church, and it is the church, His body, which receives it when administered. Private masses were carried out with the Roman Catholic docrine of ex *opere operato* as well as transubstantiation. Westminster apparently felt that any private administration, even of a proper Lord's Supper, could not be divorced from the errors associated with a private administration of the Roman Catholic mass.

29.4 Here wrong practices are listed: private masses, withholding the cup, and worshiping or adoring the elements.

The condemnation of private masses, implicit in the previous section, is made explicit here.

Withholding the cup from the laity developed in the Middle Ages after much controversy and has continued in the Roman Church to the present. It is condemned here because Christ administered both bread and cup to those first believers. If it is said that they were all ministers, that would justify withholding the bread as well as the cup from lay men and women. Even Rome has never dared to withhold the whole Lord's Supper from professing Christians. Associated with the withholding of the cup was the fear of its being spilled, since it was (wrongly, of course) supposed to become the actual blood of Jesus Christ. In other words this deprivation of the people of God was based in large part on the further and even more serious error of transubstantiation.

Acts (e.g. elevation of the host) as well as doctrines are condemned, because actions speak louder than words. The words themselves condemn. But even if the words are denied, how can the actions be denied which assume the deity of the object? Most Protestants are not guilty of this error, but their actions sometimes show that they do not always practice what they preach. Calling the communion table an altar, with the minister facing away from the people toward God, kneeling to receive the elements — what do these declare, if not the sacredness of the object? The explanation that only the sacredness of the person, not that of the objects, is represented will not wash, unless the object is supposed to be present. That is, if a person is bowing to or otherwise adoring the body of Jesus Christ and the blood, presumably that body and blood have become present to the worshiper.

According to Roman dogma, the body and the blood of Jesus in resurrected glory are at the right hand of God in heaven. He is not adored normally, because He simply is not seen. When He is, therefore, adored in the sacrament, it is because He is believed to be corporeally present. So, whatever motivates a Roman Catholic for his idolatrous acts, it is not simply because these elements have actually become Jesus Christ's body and blood. The argument that at least Catholics are consistent — wrongly believing that Christ is corporeally present, they rightfully feel and adore His presence — actually involves another question, albeit an extremely interesting one.

That question is whether Christ *in His humanity* is to be worshiped. The orthodox doctrine is that Christ's humanity is a creature, however perfect, and therefore not to be worshiped. So, even if Christ were corporeally present in His human nature, He should not be adored in that nature. The orthodox Roman Catholic may very well argue at that point that Christ's humanity is (as the *Westminster Confession* itself teaches) inseparable from His deity, the divine person of Jesus Christ. Therefore the Romanist may say that he is worshiping the divine Christ who is corporeally present in the mass. Now, it is true that Christ's human nature is inseparable from His divine person. Wherever the human nature, there is the divine nature. No one will dispute the propriety of worshiping the deity. The Roman Catholic comes then to this explanation: he worships the divine Christ as He manifests Himself in His human nature in the mass. Were it true, of course, that the elements were transubstantiated into the body and blood of the human nature of Jesus Christ, this human nature would indeed be inseparably united with the divine, and a person certainly may, or rather ought, to worship the divine Jesus Christ. So the fundamental argument always comes back to the rejection of the doctrine of transubstantiation. Since that doctrine is false and since these elements are not transubstantiated but remain merely bread and wine, Jesus Christ is not corporeally present in the communion service any more than He is omnipresent everywhere. We worship God only where He manifests Himself in His divine nature, and since He does not do this in the mass and since the elements are not transubstantiated to His body and blood, it is an act of idolatry to give obeisance to these creaturely elements.

29.5 Here again is the SACRAMENTAL UNION (27.2) between the things signified and the things themselves – this time between the elements of the Lord's Supper and what they represent. As Calvin indicates, the sacrament is one thing, its efficacy something else. There is no change in the elements themselves but only in their significance before and after their dedication to sacramental use. But the sacrament is not empty of efficacy. Ultimately, the ability of sacramental action to convey the grace of the presence of Christ depends upon the Holy Spirit, who enables the sacraments to be efficacious and is the cause of their being fruitful in the lives of believers.

29.6 Probably the most controversial words in history, certainly in theological history, are "this is my body" (Lk 22.19), specifically the word "is," which may be taken either literally or figuratively with two different interpretations for each. The literal leads to the doctrines of (1) transubstantiation of the elements into the substance of the body and blood of Christ (Roman Catholic) or (2) consubstantiation, in which the elements co-exist alongside the body and blood of Christ (Lutheran). The figurative construction sees communion either as (1) a memorial of what has happened in the past (early Zwingli) or (2) a dynamic happening in the present which communicates the effects of the past sacrifice (Calvinistic, Reformed).

This section condemns the transubstantiational interpretation for four reasons: it is said to be contrary to (1) Scripture, (2) reason, (3) common sense, and (4) the nature of the sacrament itself. It is charged with being contrary to the Scripture in a somewhat circular way, because the figurative interpretation is assumed to be the only possible one. It is against reason, because reason teaches that two bodies cannot be in two places at the same time (in heaven and on an altar). It is against common sense, because we taste bread and wine, not flesh and blood. It is against the nature of the sacrament, because that celebrates the once-for-all sacrifice of Christ and not a repetition of that sacrifice.

Consequently the doctrine of transubstantiation substitutes superstition for truth and encourages a gross and abominable idolatory which adores and worships bread and wine rather than the living God.

29.7 Here is the Reformed effort to do justice to the the Lord's Supper (while avoiding the idolatry of Roman Catholicism) by interpreting the sacrament as a spiritual partaking of Christ through the instrumentality of physical and representative objects. Thus believers FEED ON CHRIST CRUCIFIED spiritually by means of the physical representatives of His death. This does justice to the sacrifice by recognizing the genuine bodily sacrifice in the material objects used in the ceremony, while not falling into idolatry but truly receiving Christ spiritually. This has been called the dynamic theory originally taught by Peter Vermigli, Martin Bucer, and especially John Calvin. It denies any corporeal presence as taught by Catholicism and Lutheranism or any *mere* representative presence as taught by the early Zwingli. Christ is truly present and not merely represented, although not corporeally but spiritually and dynamically by His divine power as a fruit of His corporeal sacrifice.

29.8 The ignorant and wicked who partake of the Lord's Supper do so wickedly and so defile it and damn themselves. All the wicked do, of course, is to eat bread and drink wine. But since the Table is only for worthy receivers, i.e. true believers, the wicked and ignorant partakers incur the wrath of God and especially so, because this is the most wonderful representation of the grace of God. Consequently no non-believer should ever be allowed to partake of communion but should be "excommunicated." Calvin almost lost his life barring certain wicked Genevans from partaking of the Lord's Supper and thus eating and drinking their own damnation. He risked his temporal life to save the eternal lives of those transgressors, who, being wicked, resented his efforts on their behalf.

Chapter 30

Concerning Condemnation by the Church

Christ, the head of the church, has appointed ecclesiastical officers to have the KEYS to admit or bar persons from Christ's kingdom, and therefore church officers have great value for: (1) reclaiming offenders, (2) deterring others, (3) purging some, (4) vindicating the honor of Christ and the gospel, and (5) preventing the wrath of God. The administration of these functions is to take three forms: (a) admonition, (b) suspension from the Lord's Supper, and (c) excommunication from the church.

30.1 Just as God has ordained the powers that be for civil government, so His Son has appointed officers to govern His church. The *Confession* does not deem it necessary here to point out that church government is fallible, just as civil government is, and that those under both must on occasion obey God rather than men. The Head of the church was once put out of it by His governors and even crucified by them as a usurper. He still often is. Nevertheless, the divinely appointed government continues and is to be obeyed.

30.2 The KEYS OF THE KINGDOM empower officers to free people from the guilt of sin, keep the impenitent in it or withdraw the barrier when they become repentant.

The *Confession* speaks in unqualified terms of Christ's original deliverance of the keys. On the surface it sounds just as absolute as Roman Catholic authority wrongly does and as Jesus rightly did. One might expect some qualifications somewhere in this chapter, but they do not occur. Therefore we have to supply what apparently was assumed by the Westminster divines. These keys are used in accordance with the commandment of the one who gave them. Just as they were delivered to Peter on the occasion of his confession of Christ as the Son of God (Mt 16.13ff), so Peter and the other apostles (Mt 18.15ff) and all ministerial successors may and must use them according to the revealed will of God. Otherwise they cannot be obeyed and must be rejected as human usurpation of divine right.

When martyred Savonarola was condemned by the Roman Catholic authorities at his burning in Florence with the words: "we cut you off from the church militant here and from the church triumphant hereafter," he replied: "you may cut me off from the church militant here but not from the church triumphant hereafter." Similarly, the church's "authority" cut off their Lord, Jesus, from the church militant here in this world, but He ascended, continuing to rule the church triumphant in heaven and to direct the church militant on earth.

Properly exercised, the keys declare freedom from the guilt of sin or bondage to it, thus opening or closing heaven as occasion demands. Clearly this authority must be respected, since in its proper exercise it does visibly and vividly show the judgment of God from heaven.

30.3 Here the reasons for and results of church discipline are listed: (1) reclamation (of serious offenders), (2) insulation (of others from the same offenses), (3) purgation (of those who would otherwise continue to contaminate the body of Christ), (4) vindication (of the honor of Christ), and (5) salvation (from the wrath of God which would otherwise come on the contaminated body). Since today church censors are almost everywhere non-existent, it is sobering to contemplate the reclamation, insulation, purgation, vindication, and salvation that are lost thereby. As candlesticks are being steadily and regularly removed from erstwhile Christian churches (Rv 2), no one need wonder why. Most churches which have lapsed into apostasy have done so without even noticing it, because no counter measures to prevent the fatal lapse have been made in the form of church censures. An uncensored church may quickly become no church at all.

The list here begins with reclamation and ends with salvation, for sinners are not reclaimed, if they are not going to be saved. God is not mocked; whatever a man sows that shall he reap (Gal 6.7) in the next world, if not in this. If we in the church would judge ourselves now, we would not need to be judged then (1 Cor 11.31). If we do not judge now, we must be judged then.

30.4 This chapter ends with the steps to be taken in the healthy administration by church censors: admonition, suspension, and excommunication. All of these steps, of course, have their proper Biblical authority, shown in the proof texts. The church knows what to do, but she is today not doing it. Frequently in books of church order disciplinary procedures are spelled out in complete detail, but almost never taken in practice. In most churches now a person is likely to be improperly disciplined should he attempt the proper discipline, which he and those who discipline him have vowed to take.

Church discipline is one of the three essential marks of the church, along with preaching of the word and administration of the sacraments. Preaching continues, although it is rarely now full preaching of the word; the sacraments are always administered, although frequently improperly; church discipline hardly ever happens, even improperly.

Proper discipline, aiming at reclamation and salvation, follows gracious and gradual steps. First there is admonition. This warning is in private at first, and only becomes public if absolutely necessary. The admonition, private if possible, goes on to suspension, only if the same sin is persisted in or another form of more serious sin is committed. Adding suspension from the Lord's Table is hoped to be only temporary without loss of brotherhood status. Only on the incorrigible or most grave offenders does excommunication from table and fellowship occur. Even that can be overcome by true penitence and bringing forth the fruits thereof to the glory of Jesus Christ.

Chapter 31

Concerning Synods and Councils

Assemblies or synods ought to be held as needed by those Christ has put in charge to govern well for the good of the church. They are to decide on controversies and other matters of conscience and polity. These decisions are restricted to ecclesiastical questions, and, since they are made according to Scripture, must be obeyed, although not as final authority in faith and life, since councils may err.

31.1 Individual churches need advice, and therefore church leaders should call synods to get that advice and settle problems. Two assumptions here are that questions will arise and that more than local wisdom will be required to resolve them. Rather than grounding the need for synods on any Biblical mandate, the *Confession* seems here to rest its point on common sense, although assigning the responsibility for calling such meetings to the Biblically appointed leaders of individual churches is certainly implied by the Biblical requirement for church leaders actively to promote the good of the church. The principle of special calling of synods as specific needs and problems arise is based on Acts 15 (the basic proof text for paragraph 1), where the Council of Jerusalem was called for just one purpose and no time was appointed for a subsequent meeting.

31.2 Three specific functions of regularly scheduled synods are listed here: (a) to settle controversies of faith, (b) to establish administrative rules for worship and church government, and (c) to adjudicate complaints of maladministration. The focus here on purely ecclesiastical matters would seem to exclude attention to political, economic, and other secular questions outside the church's own domain. This common-sense approach is, of course, not at all common today.

The resulting pronouncements are to be obeyed, if they conform to Scripture and come from Biblically ordained authority—clearly a question left up to the judgment of individual consciences. The *Confession* here gives no directions or suggestions about what happens, when an individual does not agree that a synod's decision is Biblical. There are several possibilities, of course, which are illustrated by some contemporary issues.

Take the ordination of women to eldership and ministry, which many feel is not Biblical. Those who hold the dissenting position may choose to remain in their denominations while continuing to express their disagreement. But, if the denomination should then make assent to such ordination a prerequisite to ordination and installation, the dissenters would have to leave the denomination or their ministry. Such has occurred widely in the Presbyterian Church (U. S. A.). On the other hand, a denomination may permit dissenters to remain, if they do not foment strife. In that case those who disagree must decide how important the issue is and whether they should remain under those conditions.

31.3 All such assemblies are still made up of fallible human beings who can make mistakes, and consequently their opinions can never have the status of FINAL AUTHORITY IN MATTERS OF FAITH AND LIVING. When Luther debated the Roman Catholic champion, John Eck, at Leipzig, he concluded that the Council at Constance (1414-18) had indeed erred in condemning John Huss. The individual is always thrown back on his own private judgment to which he must ultimately conform—as Luther learned at Worms a century after Huss.

Of course, the individual's judgment may err as well. However, it is one's own judgment that one *must* follow, because it is as individuals that we must answer to our Judge. It goes without saying that the individual should initially trust the judgment of the highest official court of the church above his own individual opinion. But, should one become humbly convinced that the council is wrong, he cannot obey what he thinks is the decision of man against what he thinks is the will of God. So the decisions of councils or synods are to be an AID to standing before God and not a foundation on which to stand. They should help Christians to stand, but they cannot be substitutes for each one's own standing.

31.4 Here the point is explicitly made that ecclesiastical councils are to concern themselves with ecclesiastical and not civil questions, EXCEPT IN EXTRAORDINARY CASES OF MODEST PETITIONS OR IN AN ADVISORY CAPACITY PROMPTED BY RELIGIOUS CONSCIENCE, WHEN REQUESTED BY CIVIL AUTHORITIES. This position seems reasonable, since a body of experts in one area would not normally be equally competent or authoritative in other areas outside their expertise. We would not normally expect ecclesiastical specialists to deliver authoritative judgments on economics, politics, military techniques, foreign policy, etc. Many modern clergymen, of course, not only feel competent but well positioned to advise experts in these fields.

Nevertheless, there are times when church councils should address issues, superficially at least, outside of their ecclesiastical expertise. The cases are, however, EXTRAORDINARY. The ecclesiastical opinions on these issues should take the form of MODEST PETITIONS when originating within ecclesiastical councils on their own initiative and be prompted by CONSCIENCE, when made in response to the requests for advice BY CIVIL AUTHORITIES. Many church bodies today deliver themselves on ordinary, everyday issues in anything but a modest manner, and in the context of having frequently been requested *not* to interfere in matters outside their domain.

Chapter 32

Concerning the Condition of Man after Death and the Resurrection of the Dead

At the point of death righteous souls go immediately to heaven. The wicked go immediately to hell. (There are no other places for departed souls.) At the last day, the end of time, all the souls of the deceased, righteous and wicked, will be reunited with their bodies.

32.1 At death our souls are separated from our bodies and go into what is called the intermediate state of blessedness with God in heaven or an intermediate state of torment in hell. Moody once said,

Someday you'll read in the obituaries that D. L. Moody is dead. Don't believe a word of it. I will have only just begun to live.

He was right, if he was what he and the world thought him to be. THE SOULS OF THE RIGHTEOUS ARE THEN PERFECTED IN HOLINESS AND ARE RECEIVED INTO THE HIGHEST HEAVENS. They leave, as another Christian has said, the land of the dying and go to the land of the living. That is why for Paul "to die is gain" (Phil 1.21).

On the other hand, since it is appointed to man once to die and then the judgment (Heb 8.29), the wicked are immediately sentenced to hell, where they now exist in their disembodied state. Those who foolishly say that the only hell is here in this world will have the terrible realization, when they die, that the worst earthly existence was heaven by comparison. In hell THEY ARE SET APART FOR THE GREAT DAY OF JUDGMENT, and that makes hell more hellish, because those wicked spirits now in hell realize that they are going to be reunited with their hideous bodies and suffer in them also. By the same token those in heaven are made happier by knowing that the time is coming when their glorious bodies will be resurrected and they will enjoy heaven in them as well.

32.2 Here is the Reformed rapture, when all those who are living at the return of Christ will be raised immediately after the bodies of the dead have been resurrected and reunited with their souls. The Reformed and Biblical rapture differs in several ways from the dispensational rapture: (1) it occurs generally at the return of Christ to judge the whole world and not secretly to separate believers; (2) it therefore is a rapture or catching up of the wicked as well as the righteous; and (3) it is the immediate prelude to the last judgment, which is described in the last chapter of the *Confession*. The fact that Paul *speaks only* of the rapture of the saved in 1 Thessalonians 4 does not mean that *only* the saints are raptured at that time. The saved happen to be all Paul discusses in that passage. The Bible teaches the joint rapture of all mankind, dead and living, at the second coming of Christ (see Mt 16.27, 25.31-32, and Jn 5.28.29).

There are both a difference and a sameness about the bodies of the resurrected, saved and unsaved alike. That is, there is a continuity, so that we will have the same bodies as those we had on earth, but, these new bodies will have DIFFERENT CHARACTERISTICS, fitting them for eternal existence in heaven or hell. They are UNITED . . . WITH THEIR SOULS FOREVER, because man is by nature a body-soul being. Consequently the Bible speaks of the intermediate state as one in which the souls of the saved long to be "clothed" in their resurrected bodies (2 Cor 5.2) and, by implication, the wicked loathe to be clothed with theirs

32.3 At the resurrection Christ fashions THE BODIES OF THE UNJUST TO DISHONOR and those of the JUST TO HONOR (like His own glorious body). Here is the story of Dorian Gray to perfection — bodies to match souls. Dorian's soul is evil, as all the souls of the wicked are, and will have a body to match.

Believers' souls will be as glorious as Christ's by whose merit they have been made so.

We all recognize the appropriateness of bodies to match souls. Beautiful spirits should be in beautiful bodies, as is often not the case in this world. Ugly spritis should be in ugly bodies, as is also often not the case in this world. Although inner beauty tends to make the body shine and inner ugliness to make the expression ugly, there is no perfect match of the exterior to the interior now. This section points out that what is now only a tendency will be perfected in the future resurrection.

Chapter 33

Concerning the Last Judgment

The Day of Judgment will take place under Jesus Christ, before whom all APOSTATE ANGELS and all men will appear to give a total account of themselves — not to inform Christ but as the occasion for Him to reveal His glory in judgment, as He brings the righteous to everlasting life and the wicked to everlasting damnation. God wants us to know about this coming day so as to deter the wicked from wickedness and to make the righteous morally alert and eager for His coming.

33.1 Although God the Father ORDAINED this day, God the Son is the judge of it. On this day every man and some angels will give account of everything that they have thought, said, and done. Elect angels are not mentioned, because they have already been judged and are established in holiness. This is true of elect humans also, but only with reference to their disembodied state after death on earth, which is not their complete, final, or perfected state. Consequently further judgment or vindication is necessary for them. Yet the APOSTATE ANGELS are to be judged then, although they have been judged already in the only state (spiritual) in which they ever exist. The reason is that they have been allowed to affect the earth and will be judged accordingly and thereafter never allowed to be free of the bottomless pit and the everlasting chains. One wonders, of course, why the good angels will not be rewarded for all the good they have done from the fall of man to the Day of Judgment.

Everyone will appear together at the Day of Judgment. There will be no separation before the judgment of the good and evil from the raptured. They will give an account of everything —

THOUGHTS, WORDS, AND ACTIONS—and be judged for everything good or evil in thought or action. As Jesus says, "every idle word will be brought into judgment" (Mt 12.36), and every cup of cold water will have its reward (Mt 10.42).

33.2 The Day of Judgment especially displays THE GLORY OF HIS MERCY and THE GLORY OF HIS JUSTICE. His mercy brings the elect to life, and His justice brings the wicked to ETERNAL TORMENT. All things are for the glory of God—and, as we have seen above, for the benefit of those who appreciate it. The Day of Judgment is no exception. Perhaps it is the greatest display of God's mercy and justice. On that day His mercy is declared forever to the saints, and the justice of His wrath is likewise eternal. Thus, it is the infinite glory of God that altogether justifies heaven and hell. Indeed, it more than justifies them, because, although they are everlasting, they are not from eternity, and no creature is capable either of the infinite fullness of mercy or the infinite fullness of justice. But this is the closest approximation possible for any creature.

Between the lines, the *Confession* shows that justice obtains where mercy is infinite by noting that it is not only the elect but the RIGHTEOUS who go into everlasting life and that it is not only the non-elect but the WICKED who go deservedly into ETERNAL TORMENT. The wicked are guilty of the sin of not knowing or obeying God, and there is only one proper treatment of sin: eternal death.

Curiously the *Confession* suggests that the wicked in hell are AWAY FROM THE PRESENCE OF THE LORD AND THE GLORY OF HIS POWER. They are indeed away from the *saving* presence of the Lord, but even then not away from THE GLORY OF HIS POWER, which is precisely what causes their ETERNAL TORMENT. His presence *is* the terror of the Lord; nothing is so frightful as the wrath of the Lamb.

33.3 In the previous section the ultimate reasons are given for the Day of Judgment. In this section we have the present reasons for knowledge about the Day of Judgment. These reasons are: to deter sin; to console the suffering godly; to prevent fleshly, worldly security; and to promote alertness and readiness for the Day of Judgment, which is in the indefinite distance but also has a very present relevance. Its future, absolute certainty affects us here and now.

The Day of Judgment deters sin, because it asks what does it profit a man if he gain the whole (present) world and lose his own soul (at the Day of Judgment). No man, remembering the certainty of impending judgment will commit the folly of sole preoccupation with the here and now, nor will Christians consider present suffering "worthy to be compared" with the glory which is to follow at the Day of Judgment and after. Nor is anyone going to be carnally secure when carnal things are precisely what will be weighed and found wanting at the Day of Judgment. When someone says that he will live one world at a time and let the future take care of itself, we know that he does not believe in the Day of Judgment. Jesus calls such people fools (Lk 12.18ff).

Chapter 34

Of the Holy Spirit

Chapters 34 and 35 are American supplements to the original *Westminster Confession of Faith*. They were added by PCUSA in 1904. Later in this century PCUS adopted them as well, putting them as new Chapters 9 and 10 and renumbering the subsequent chapters.

In Chapter 34 we are taught that the Holy Spirit is the third person of the Trinity, who, being the same substance and equal with the Father and the Son, is the source of all good and the inspirer of Scripture. He is especially active in the gospel dispensation, which He prepared for, and He urges the message in the hearts of men, regenerating, persuading, uniting, sanctifying, and adopting believers into Christ. He thus unites believers to one another in the church, calling many to serve as officers, and "by him the church will be preserved, increased, purified, and at last made perfectly holy in the presence of God."

34.1 In this section the full deity and equality of the Holy Spirit is affirmed. This affirmation of the orthodox view of the person of the Holy Spirit is strangely lacking in the original *Westminster Confession*. It is also helpful to be reminded here that the Holy Spirit is to be worshiped, since the church tends to address almost always the Father, rarely the Son, and almost never the Holy Spirit. This is no doubt because He is the one who leads us to pray to the Father in the name of the Son. Although these distinctions in the *economic* Trinity are true and appropriately recognized, that does not exclude the truth of the *essential* Trinity, according to which the Holy Spirit is truly and fully God and therefore worthy of worship as much as the Father or the Son.

34.2 The role of applying the holiness of God to individuals, whether to believers in the process of sanctification or to non-believers, is the emphasis of this section. One can see why the Southern Presbyterian Church (PCUS) placed this chapter after Chapter 8 on the mediatorial work of Christ, because the Holy Spirit is the great applier of the work of Christ the Mediator to the hearts of people.

While the chapter on EFFECTUAL CALLING (10) teaches that the Holy Spirit is the author of regeneration, this chapter adds that He works with many who are never regenerated, but that in resisting the merciful offers of the gospel, they are guilty of "resisting the Holy Spirit." Therefore, although man is passive in regeneration, as Chapter 10 shows, here it is observed that man is very active in resisting the work of the Spirit of God.

This section of Chapter 34 also properly notes that the Holy Spirit is active before regeneration as well as in and after it, as He urges the gospel "upon the reason and conscience of men." This is also a useful addition to Chapter 1 by calling attention to the fact that the Holy Spirit is the one who inspired the writers of Holy Scripture "to record infallibly the mind and will of God."

34.3 The otherwise fine doctrinal tribute to the work of the Holy Spirit in this chapter becomes problematical in the order of statements in this section. The very first assertion is that God "is ever willing to give [the Holy Spirit] to all who ask him." The second sentence goes on to state that the Holy Spirit "regenerates men by his grace . . .," etc. This would appear to mean that some people ask for the Spirit before they are regenerated. If so, we have an Arminian or even Pelagian error, contrary to Psalm 110.3 and John 1.12, for example, and to the whole teaching of the original *Westminster Confession*. Although God is willing to give His Spirit "to all who ask Him," only those ask Him to whom God has given the regenerating Spirit. "In the day of the Lord's power the people shall be willing" (Ps 110.3).

It is also clear that the Spirit "regenerates by His grace." However, this regeneration does not follow men's receiving Him, but rather precedes that reception. With these qualifications then we have a fine statement here of the internal work of the Spirit of God. We note with pleasure that repentance and faith are presented as following regeneration, and the strong statement, "enables them to embrace Jesus Christ by faith," is pure and soundly orthodox Reformed teaching.

34.4 This section considers the "indwelling of the Holy Spirit" in all believers as essential to and constituitive of the church and her work. The union of believers with Christ is the work of the Holy Spirit. If union with Christ is the foundation of all blessings, the Holy Spirit is the foundation of this union. In Christ we have all things, and in the Holy Spirit we have Christ. The Spirit is also the tie that binds our hearts together in Christian love. Just as truly as the Holy Spirit is the eternal love-bond between Father and Son in the blessed Trinity, so He is between one regenerate member of the body of Christ and every other. The whole body of Christ is built up in Christ to maturity by the energy of the Spirit of Christ.

From Him also come the ministers and other officers who lead the church in this holy vocation. It is the work of the Holy Spirit who leads the church to press on to her high calling in Christ Jesus and gives her the leaders to help reach that divine goal. Not only are the men who administer the word and the ordinances appointed by the Spirit, but He makes these ordinances to be efficacious. Probably this section does not mean that He literally gives or bestows efficacy on the ordinances, but rather that He Himself works efficiently by and through them.

So, the ultimate goal of a perfect church, which was purchased by Christ and built up by His servants (Eph 4.11-13) will at last "be made perfectly holy" by the Holy Spirit.

Chapter 35

Of the Gospel of the Love of God and Missions

This chapter, also added in 1904 by the PCUSA and subsequently adopted by the PCUS (with the briefer title, "Of the Gospel"), essentially reflects orthodox Reformed doctrine with one important exception.

35.1 The first section states that God has provided a great sufficiency for the salvation of all men and freely offers it to them. Here the classical formula about the gospel in its relationship to mankind (the gospel is sufficient for all but only efficient for some) is slightly altered in that only the first half is reiterated – that the gospel is sufficient for all and offered to all. By not stating that Christ's sacrifice, although of infinite value and able to save all men, is savingly applied only to the elect, this section allows the view that God intends the salvation through Christ for every human.

35.2 Here the hint becomes the plain assertion that God desires all men to be saved. Not only is this not true, but it is contrary to everything else the *Westminster Confession* says about this subject. If God desires to save all men, why doesn't He do so? It is God who elects some, not all (Chp 3), sends His mediator for the elect, not for all men (Chp 8), and gives regeneration to some, passive men, not to all (Chp 10). That is because He desires to save those whom He elected to salvation, sends His Son to die for their salvation, and His Holy Spirit to bring them to salvation. If God had desired to save all,

He would have elected all, the Son would have died for all, and the Spirit of God would have regenerated all.

Various texts are often cited to support the notion of God's desiring the salvation of all men. Three deserve brief comment here. The first is 1 Timothy 2.4, where it is said that God "desires all men to be saved." But the verb *thelo* does not always means desire. It can mean "will" or "command." If God desired all men to be saved, while many actually perish, then the ever-blessed God would be the ever-miserable God. Furthermore, the Greek *pan* ("all") does not necessarily mean each and every but can, for example, refer to all the kinds or classes of people mentioned in the context. The last reference in the context of this passage is to Christians, that they may lead a peaceful life (4.2), So the statement must mean that God desires that all the elect be saved. The same "all" (*pan*) shows up with a different Greek word for will in 2 Peter 3.9, where God is said to be "unwilling that any should perish but that all should come to repentance" (AV). Here the context clearly shows that Peter is referring only to the elect, for they are the ones who "come to repentance," because God grants them repentance (2 Tm 2.25).

Finally, the familiar John 3.16 teaches that God's saving love for the world is for the world of the elect, because they and only they are those who "believe." God so loved the world that He gave His only Son that whoever believes (i.e. the elect) should not perish. The passage asserts that God gave His Son for the elect throughout the whole world.

35.3 Back on track again, this section points out that it is the duty and privilege of everyone to accept the gospel and that failure to do so is each person's "own fault." While election and regeneration account for faith and salvation, it is sin that accounts for unbelief and guilt and hence the proper conclusion that unbelief is the sinner's "own fault." Belief comes from the new heart which is the gracious gift of God to those for whom Christ died and purchased salvation. Unbelief comes from the old wicked heart with which all of Adam's descendants are born and which they never choose to repudiate on their own. Rather they cleave to their old nature in spite of the gracious offers of the gospel to all who believe.

We are reminded from the chapter on free will (9) that the choice of unbelief or the refusal to believe is from the person himself. God restrains no one from Christ. Each sinful human does his or her own restraining of self from confessing sins and coming to the Savior of all who do confess their sins. Now it is true that sinful humans, trapped in and with a sinful heart, cannot do otherwise than reject the gospel unless the Father "draws" them (Jn 6.44), but that amounts to the same thing as rejecting the gospel on their own. It is therefore entirely each sinner's fault for not accepting Christ. God is not to be blamed for sin, when, in fact, as Augustine and Edwards observe, sin is only committed in the absence of God.

35.4 This last statement of the *Westminster Confession*, including the insights of the twentieth-century as well as the seventeenth, shows that, contrary to inhibiting evangelism, the Reformed faith leads directly to it. Just as Christ commands His disciples to make disciples in all the world, so the church is responsible for extending His kingdom "throughout the whole earth." The election of Chapter 3 leads to the evangelism of Chapter 35. Paul, the greatest missionary of all time, endured all things for the sake of the elect (2 Tm 2.10).

One way alone ("there is no other way") is the foundation of world missions. There is no other name than Christ's under heaven whereby men may be saved (Acts 4.12). World missions is the job for all Christians under the inspired directions of the New Testament. This includes the home front where Christians "contribute by their prayers, gifts, and personal efforts to the extension of the kingdom of Christ throughout the whole earth."

This work of the Holy Spirit completes the divine Trinity's plan of salvation, as John Murray, probably our century's finest Reformed theologian, has so well shown in his *Redemption Accomplishied and Applied*. So now we see the whole trinal redemption: God allocates it; the Son accomplishes it; the Spirit applies it. Amen. Allelulia!

Declaratory Statement

Here is an addition by PCUSA meant only to disavow "certain inferences" illegitimately drawn from the *Confession*. Its first paragraph interprets the meaning of Chapter 3 on God's eternal decrees, and the second interprets the third section on ELECT INFANTS in Chapter 10 (CONCERNING EFFECTUAL CALLING).

First of all it is declared that Chapter 3's eternal decree is in harmony with: (1) God's [benevolent] love to "all mankind", (2) His willingness to give salvation to all who seek it, (3) His not desiring that any should perish, (4) His providing salvation sufficient for and adapted to all, (5) His "gracious" offering to all, (6) His decree hindering "no man from accepting the gospel," and (7) the condemnation of none except by his or her own sin. All these statements, except the third (see the remarks above on 35.2), are true as taught by the Scriptures and specifically those that use the scriptural language. There is, however, probably a wrong intention behind the occasionally ambiguous language which seems intent on equivocating about the whole doctrine of God's sovereign election. Warfield opposed these statements simply because they make ambiguous a creed noted for its clarity and precision.

The second paragraph here actually changes 10.3. The "Declaratory Statement" asserts that "it is not to be received as teaching that any who die in infancy are lost." The original Section 3 of the *Confession* only says that "some" infants are elect. The normal implication is that therefore some others are not elect, and, of course, according to the *Confession* all die in Adam and are lost *unless* and *if* elected to be saved in Christ — in which category there are only "some" infants. By stretching "some" into "all" the "Declaratory Statement" misrepresents the probable meaning of the original 10.3. The Westminster divines certainly did not declare that all dying in infancy are elect. On the other hand the wishful thinking reflected in the PCUSA's hopeful interpretation was probably shared by the Westminster Assembly. They probably *hoped,* as we all do, "that all dying in infancy are included in the election of grace."

Synoptic Outline
of the Confession

1. Holy Scripture

1. Biblical revelation:
   natural revelation of God insufficient for salvation
   Biblical revelation necessary
   once for all in Scripture
2. books of OT and NT:
   inspired by God
   rule of faith and life
3. Apocryphal books:
   not inspired
   not authoritative
4. Bible authoritative because it is God's word
5. human reasons to accept Biblical authority
   only Holy Spirit savingly convinces us
6. everything we need to know about God and our
   relationship to Him is in the Bible
   nothing to be added to the Bible
   saving understanding only by Holy Spirit
   some provisions of religion not in Bible
7. meaning of all passages not equally clear
   basic meanings can be understood by everyone
8. OT in Hebrew, NT in Greek
   Bible to be translated into every human language
9. Bible self-interpreting
10. Holy Spirit, speaking in Bible, supreme authority
    of all religious controversies, councils, teachings,
    and opinions

2. God and the Holy Trinity

1. there is only one God
2. God has all life and everything else in and of Himself
   He must be worshiped as God

3. there are three persons in the Godhead, the Father,
   the Son (eternally generated from the Father),
   and the Holy Spirit (eternally coming from the
   Father and the Son)

3. God's Eternal Decrees

1. God has ordained all things from all eternity
2. but not because He foresaw that they would happen
3. He has predestined some humans to everlasting life
   He has foreordained the rest to everlasting death
4. this predestination/foreordination is precise and
   unchangeable
5. out of His mercy and grace (and not because of
   anything they would do) God chose those
   predestined to life to be in Christ
6. He also ordained all the means by which they should
   come to and stay in Christ
7. God decided to demonstrate His mere justice on
   everybody else (the unsaved)

4. Creation

1. the triune God made everything in the world in six days
2. God made human beings, male and female, last
   with knowledge, righteousness, and true holiness
   in His own image
   with His law in their hearts
   with freedom of will
   they were commanded not to eat of Tree of Knowledge
   of Good and Evil

5. Providence

1. according to His sovereign will, God's p. sustains
   and controls everything that happens
2. therefore God is the first cause of everything
   all secondary causes also are according to His p.
3. God works out p. daily by natural, ordinary means

uses supernatural ones whenever He wants
4. p. extends even to sin and sinning
   but God does not cause sin
5. God's p. allows believers' sin for their own ultimate good
6. God spiritually blinds the reprobate
   gives them over to their freely chosen sin
      for their own damnation
7. God takes special care of His church

6. Fall of Man, Sin, and Punishment of Sin

1. tempted by Satan, Adam and Eve sinned in eating
   the forbidden fruit
2. they became spiritually dead in sin and completely polluted
3. the same condition (original sin) happens to all humans
   as the descendants and heirs of Adam
4. in this condition humans are totally inclined to evil
   and disinclined to good
   from this condition all actual sins proceed
5. this corrupt nature remains (in this life) even in the saved
6. every sin, original and actual, incurs God's wrath
   or chastening

7. God's Covenant with Man

1. distance between God and man so great that God
   provided covenants for man
2. the first c., with Adam, was a c. of works
3. The second is the c. of grace, salvation through Christ
4. the Bible identifies c. of grace as a testament
5. OT c. of grace was administered under the
   dispensation of the law
6. NT c. of grace under the dispensation of the gospel

8. Christ the Mediator

1. God chose and ordained Jesus to save men
2. Jesus truly God and truly man
3. Uniting but not confusing God and man, Jesus

completely equipped as mediator
4. as such, Jesus: fulfilled law, suffered, died, buried,
      resurrected, ascended into heaven, intercedes,
      will judge
5. Jesus' sacrifice fully satisfied God's justice
6. true believers before Christ saved by Him
7. sometimes Bible attributes to Jesus' human nature
      what belongs to His divine nature and vice versa
8. Christ Himself effectively calls and saves all the elect

9. Free Will

1. man's will is free
2. prelapsarian man could naturally will and do what
      pleases God
3. fallen man will not and so is hopelessly dead in sin
4. on conversion, God gives the new person the inclination
      to will and do what is spiritually good
   the old nature remains as well
5. only in state of glory is man's will perfectly inclined to do
      only good

10. Effectual Calling

1. God effectually calls the elect at the right time
   they come to Christ voluntarily
2. God does this out of His own will and not because
      of anything the sinner does or ever will do
3. elect infants dying in infancy are saved
   so are other elect who have not heard gospel
4. all others, those not chosen, are damned

11. Justification

1. the imputation of Christ's obedience and judicial
      satisfaction to each believer
2. faith is the means of j.
3. Christ fully discharges the debt of the justified

4. elect are justified when Holy Spirit actually applies
Christ to them, in time
5. God continues to forgive the sins of the justified
6. j. same in OT and NT

12. Adoption

1. the justified are adopted by God as His children

13. Sanctification

1. in s. saved are empowered by Christ to conquer
the sinfulness of their old natures
2. s. works in whole person but not completely in this life
old self continues to battle the Spirit
3. old nature wins battles, but Spirit of Christ enables
believers to grow spiritually

14. Saving Faith

1. s.f. is a gift from God worked by the Holy Spirit in the
hearts of the elect
aided by the word, prayer, and sacraments
2. consequently elect believe the Bible and accept Christ
3. different degrees of s.f.

15. Repentance Leading to Life

1. product of gospel working in believers' lives
2. involves seeing sin as God does,
turning away from sins to walk with God
3. r. sine qua non of forgiveness
4. size of sin does not affect r.
5. repent of sins specifically
6. confession necessary
privately to God
publicly as appropriate to those wronged

16. Good Works

1. only those identified and commanded by God
2. believers do them in obedience to God
3. believers enabled to do them by the Holy Spirit
4. believers never do more than God requires
5. do not merit salvation
6. are accepted and rewarded by God in Christ
7. by nonbelievers do not please God
   nonbelievers better off doing them than not

17. Perseverance of God's People

1. once saved, always saved
2. result of God's unchangeable election, Christ's merit
   and intercession, indwelling Spirit, and nature of
   covenant of grace
3. believers can neglect these means of their
   preservation and for a time draw away from God

18. Assurance of Grace and Salvation

1. unsaved can deceive themselves that they are saved
   saved can be fully assured in this life
2. because of: divine promises, inner awareness, witness
   and seal of Holy Spirit
3. believers can have doubts
   should seek full assurance
4. a. may be shaken but is never completely lost

19. Law of God

1. God gave to Adam
   promised life in keeping it, death in not
2. same law in ten commandments, perfect rule of
   righteousness
3. For Jews before Christ ordinances and ceremonial
   laws added
   these are nullified in the NT

4. Jews also given judicial laws which may or may not be
    used by subsequent civil governments
5. moral law pertains to everyone, saved and unsaved
    gospel strengthens its authority
6. law is useful for believers
7. agrees with the gospel

20. Christian Freedom and Freedom of Conscience

1. c.f. purchased by Christ in OT and NT, from: curse of
    moral law, evil world, enslavement to Satan,
    dominion of sin, evil of afflictions, sting of death,
    victory of grave, and everlasting damnation
    gives free access to God
    in NT added freedom from OT ceremonial law, greater
    access to throne of grace, and fuller gift of Holy Spirit
2. God only Lord of conscience
3. practicing sin is antithetical to c.f.
4. civil and religious authorities established by God to
    uphold c.f.
    therefore, those who oppose either shoud be called
    to account by the church

21. Religious Worship and the Sabbath Day

1. natural understanding shows there is a God
    God should be worshiped according to His rules in
    the Bible
2. triune God is to be worshiped
    but not anyone or anything else
    worship must involve a mediator (the only one is Christ)
3. prayer is part of worship
    must be in Jesus' name, according to God's will, and
    in a known tongue
4. prayer is for the living or yet to live
    not for the dead
    not for those having committed the sin unto death

5. worship includes: reading Bible, sound preaching
    and attentive hearing, psalm singing, and sacraments
    plus oaths, vows, and fasting
6. God is to be worshiped everywhere
    public worship with fellow believers not to be neglected
7. one day in seven holy to God
    before Christ the last day of week
    since then the first
8. proper sabbath: prepared for, resting from worldly
    works and recreation, spending on worship and
    charitable works (and necessities)

22. Lawful Oaths and Vows

1. l.o. part of worship
    are proper to take
2. swear only by God's name
    take an oath when lawfully required
3. swear seriously only to what is true
    sinful to refuse to take an oath required by lawful authority
4. use plain sense of words, no equivocation
    cannot obligate one to sin
    must not be broken no matter to whom made
5. vow similar to oath
6. vows to be made only to God
7. vow nothing contrary to God's word
    and only what you can do
    monastic vows not to be made

23. Civil Authorities

1. established by God to punish wrong and promote right
2. Christians may accept public office
    should promote true religion
    may wage war
3. c.a. not to interfere in religion
    should support Christian denominations
    protect all individuals whether religious or not
4. honor and respect c.a. no matter whether Christian or not

pope has no civil authority

24. Marriage and Divorce [original]

1. m. monogamous
2. m. for mutual help of husband and wife, procreation of
holy seed, prevention of moral impurity
3. everyone physically and psychologically able may marry
Christians should marry only Christians
4. m. forbidden between family members as defined in Bible
5. adultery or fornication dissolves marriage
adultery grounds for d.
6. adultery and irremediable desertion only grounds of d.
proceedings for d. must be public and orderly

24. Marriage and Divorce [UP]

1. Christian m. est. by God for as long as husband and
wife live
2. breach of m. may occasion divorce
remarriage allowed by Bible and gospel of Christ may
be sanctioned

24. Marriage and Divorce [PC]

1. m. monogamous as long as husband and wife live
2. m. for mutual help, development of character,
propagation, rearing children as Christians
3. everyone with judgment may marry
both partners should be evangelical Christians
4. m. civil and religious
5. d. allowed by weakness of partners leading to
irremediable physical or spiritual infidelity
6. remarriage allowed when Christian intention manifest
7. divorced should consider remaining single

25. The Church

1. the universal c. consists of all the elect

    2. the visible c. consists of everyone in the world who
          professes true religion and their children
    3. visible c. enabled by Christ through ministry, Bible,
          and ordinances
    4. universal c. more or less visible
    5. purest visible churches not completely pure
       some churches synagogues of Satan
       always c. on earth
    6. Jesus only head of c.

26. Fellowship of God's People

    1. all the elect united to each other in Christ
    2. must help and support each other
    3. believers not therefore equal to Christ or to have
          property in common

27. The Sacraments

    1. holy signs and seals of covenant of grace
       represent Christ and His benefits, distinguish
          believers from everyone else, and engage believers
          to serve Christ
    2. spiritual/sacramental union of sign and thing signified
    3. grace in sacraments not from any magical power in
          them or from the person administering them but
          from the Holy Spirit working in them
    4. only two sacraments
       to be administered by ministers
    5. sacraments of OT signify same thing as those of NT

28. Baptism

    1. signifies believers coming to Christ
       to be continued to the end of the world
    2. water used in name of trinity
    3. dipping not necessary
       sprinkling sufficient
    4. infants of believing parents to be baptized

5. salvation not tied intrinsically to b.
6. effectiveness of b. not tied to time of its administration
7. each person to be baptized only once

29. The Lord's Supper

1. initiated by Christ before crucifixion as:
     perpetual remembrance of it; seal of cross's
     benefits; signification of spiritual nourishment of
     believers; and pledge of believers' communion with
     Christ and each other
2. l.s. commemorates Christ's once for all sacrifice
     does not repeat it
     Roman Catholic mass horribly misrepresents l.s.
3. ministers administer l.s. to believers who are
     present according to Biblical instructions
4. abuses of l.s.: private communions or receiving
     l.s. alone; denying the cup to the congregation;
     worshiping or adoring the bread and wine
5. bread and wine remain bread and wine
6. doctrine of transubstantiation nonsensical, denies
     true nature of sacraments
7. worthy partakers spiritually receive and feed on
     Christ crucified
8. nonbelievers must not be allowed to receive l.s.
     when they do they damn themselves

30. Condemnation by the Church

1. church government established by Christ
2. church officers have keys of kingdom
     close it to unrepentant
     open it to repentant sinners
3. church condemnation needed to: reclaim believers
     who have seriously erred; deter others from doing
     that; purge the church; vindicate the honor of Christ;
     and avoid God's wrath.
4. church officers shall: warn offenders, exclude from
     Lord's Supper, or excommunicate.

31. Synods and Councils

1. s. and c. should be held
2. to: settle religious controversies; establish rules for
       church administration; and hear complaints
   decisions should conform to Bible
3. s. and c. make and have made mistakes
   therefore they are only aids to answering questions
       of faith and living
4. s. and c. should only consider church questions
   secular opinions only at request of civil authorities

32. Man after Death and the Resurrection

1. after death of body, souls live on in either heaven or hell
2. at last day the living will be changed without
       physically dying
   all the dead will be resurrected in same bodies they had
3. bodies of unjust raised to dishonor
   of just raised to honor in pattern of Christ's body

33. The Last Judgment

1. Christ will judge all the apostate angels and all the
       human beings who ever lived
2. l.j. reveals God's glory in mercy to the elect (who
       go into everlasting life) and in justice to the unsaved
       (who will go to eternal torment and punishment).
3. Christ wants us to be convinced that there is going
       to be a day of ultimate reckoning
   but wants no one to know exactly when

34. The Holy Spirit [UP and PC]

1. third person of trinity
   to be believed in, loved, obeyed, and worshiped
2. Lord and Giver of life
   inspired Bible
   prepares way for gospel in humans

3. regenerates men, convicts of sins, moves to
    repentance, persuades and enables them to accept
    Christ, unites believers to Christ, dwells in believers,
    and seals them until the day of redemption
4. vitally unites believers to each other
  calls and anoints ministers, church officers, and
    imparts gifts to believers
  preserves and purifies the church

35. Gospel of Love of God and Missions [UP and PC]

1. g. freely offered to everyone
2. shows God commands all men to be saved
  reveals the only way of salvation
  promises eternal life
  invites and commands humans to accept Christ
3. must be accepted
4. ordinarily communicated through God's word
  therefore Christ has commanded the church to
    make disciples throughout the whole world

Declaratory Statement [UP]

Re Chp 3, the *Confession* means that all men are free to accept the gospel and that no one is condemned except by his own sin.

Re Chp 10.3, the *Confession* means that all who die in infancy are saved.

Subject Index

Index of Names